THE ARCHITECTURE OF FRANK SCHLESINGER

To Isabel & Anthony
with appreciation for your
vision

5·30·0

THE ARCHITECTURE OF FRANK SCHLESINGER

Foreword by Charles Gwathmey, FAIA
Introduction by Thomas L. Schumacher

To
Christy, for the future
and
Draga, for the past

Grayson Publishing, LLC
1250 28th Street NW
Washington, DC 20007

First Edition: May 2005

ISBN 0-9749632-3-2

Printed in Korea

CONTENTS

FOREWORD

BY CHARLES GWATHMEY, FAIA

Frank Schlesinger was my second year studio critic in 1957 at the University of Pennsylvania School of Architecture and we have been friends since.

He was young, yct had a presence. I nicknamed him Robert Mitchem. Initially, I felt insecure about him, as well as his critiques, not because he was acute, understated and perceptive, but because he was not very friendly. However, he grew on you. If he believed you were committed, worked hard and were determined to produce a rigorously consistent project, he was more open, supportive and genuinely engaged. He also revealed a wry sense of humor.

He never told you what to do nor was he interested in pictorial or stylistic solutions. He always asked the provocative question that forced you to reevaluate and/or clarify the parti. He was demanding and you felt a sense of obligation to both fulfill his expectations, as well as your own aspirations. This is what makes a motivational teacher and a contributive architect.

As I write this, it could be reinterpreted as a brief summary of his work.

Louis Kahn was the master professor at the school and his influence was pervasive, not only to his immediate students, who were reverent, but to the undergraduates and faculty, as well.

There is a clear and positive influence of Kahn in Frank's work: plan clarity; material ethic; three dimensional geometric resolution; fenestration hierarchy; spatial enrichment through the manipulation and inclusion of natural light; solidity and density in massing; and a sense of essence, reinforced by the absence of decoration–an architecture of primariness, enriched by a rigorous adherence to the formal resolution of "parti".

In Frank's oeuvre, the reoccurring parti idea, as illustrated on page 204, is the courtyard, as the referential and generating space in the building's organization.

It is classic and fundamental, but in the illustrated projects, the courtyard is constantly manipulated to accommodate and anchor both additions to existing structures, as well as new buildings.

The work supports the truism that an architect should be obligated to fully comprehend the legacy of history, both retrospectively and speculatively, as well as, the influences of context, culture and place; none of which, by the way, have anything to do with style, but everything to do with content.

One way that we understand the history of our culture and our times is through our public architecture. This history, from ancient times to the present, was never a record of preservation, but quite the opposite: a series of subtractions and additions, with an inspirational view of the future.

Institutional buildings have historically set precedents, both in design and spirit. There was a gap in mid-century modernism, of twenty or so years from the 1950's through the 1970's, when this public architecture lost its credibility, and became simply accommodative and space enclosing. Most buildings were void of meaning or content, primarily because architects ignored the lessons of history.

Frank's buildings are the exception. The most representative projects in my view that prove a continued commitment to one's conviction and ideals through the stylistic contamination of changing times, include the earlier Schlesinger Residence in Bucks County, PA; the Girl Scout Dining Hall in Quakertown, PA of the 1960s; and the later 2001 St. Francis of Assisi Parish School in Triangle, Virginia, a summary project that proves the ethic of process continuity.

Frank Schlesinger is an architect's architect. We learn from his work, are inspired, and reinvigorated by its durability, both literally and philosophically.

Charles Gwathmey is a principal of Gwathmey Siegel & Associates Architects in New York City.

INTRODUCTION

FRANK SCHLESINGER: ORIGINS/RESULTS
BY THOMAS L. SCHUMACHER

"We shall all agree that the fundamental aspect of the novel is its story-telling aspect… Yes—oh, dear, yes—the novel tells a story…. That is the highest factor common to all novels, and I wish that it was not so, that it could be something different—melody, or perception of the truth…"

E.M. Forster

"Originality means returning to origins."

Carles Vallhonrat, quoting
Louis Kahn, quoting
Antonio Gaudí

Most architectural monographs these days describe young avant-garde practitioners with a number of exciting unbuilt projects, and a few finished (mostly small) works. The books are typically highly polemical, visually extreme, and often near impossible to read; the texts and the graphics are often opaque. Presenting an architect whose career spans almost a half-century is decidedly different. In the *Architecture of Frank Schlesinger* we have mostly built-work, quite consistent over the years in its stylistic qualities, but varied in scale and program type. Schlesinger is a "modern architect" in the old sense of that term: his work represents the ethic of the early 20th century, when honesty of structural and material expression, clarity of plan and spatial organization, directness of functional response, and a logic to the design process were values that most modernists promoted.

Americans who graduated from architecture school in the decade following WWII were a special—some would say, an elite—group. Entering the profession in that period provided those architects with two benefits: first, the country experienced an unprecedented economic expansion, resulting in untold inter-esting architectural commissions. Second, most of the world witnessed the triumph of modernism as the architecture of choice in both the public and private realms. It is easy to overlook the fact that before WWII modern architecture was a niche market, and that the production of traditional buildings far outnumbered those of the modernists. The optimism amongst architects of the postwar period for architecture's social potential and for the benefits of the modern style they had mastered in the Bauhaus-influenced education system (brought to America by Gropius and Mies in the late 1930s), was infectious.

Frank Schlesinger began his career in the mid-1950s, toward the end of the first decade after the War. After service in the Navy in WWII, he had gone to Middlebury College for two years and then began his architectural studies at RPI (Troy, NY, was his home town). Schlesinger left RPI because, as an engineering school, the architecture curriculum at that time was too dry and technically oriented. He then went off to the University of Illinois, then the largest architecture school in America. (While at Illinois, Schlesinger purchased an Alvar Aalto bentwood chair which he has credited for whetting his appetite for natural materials as well as an appreciation of Scandinavian design that went way beyond Aalto.) Receiving his undergraduate degree at Illinois, he left Urbana in part because the curriculum was still heavily influenced by the *Ecole des Beaux Arts* system, but also because he had met Hideo Sasaki, who after graduating from the Harvard Graduate School of Design (GSD) was teaching at the University of Illinois Landscape Architecture Department. Schlesinger found the GSD design approach espoused by Sasaki stimulating and when Sasaki returned to Harvard to teach, Schlesinger followed him. Schlesinger followed a teacher, not a School of Thought. This pattern would continue.

At Harvard he studied with Hugh Stubbins, for whom he worked after graduation. He then went to New York City where he worked for Marcel Breuer. Breuer was the quintessential builder, always concerned with the elegant solution. He was at the apex of his professional stature and it was an exciting time to be in his, then, relatively small office (this was before Breuer's buildings began to affect the ponderous plasticity of his later style).

But Schlesinger tends to minimize those earliest influences. Philadelphia and Louis Kahn were more important. It was the late fifties and early sixties.

There are two Philadelphias. There is the serious "Main Line" Philadelphia of the "The Philadelphia Story," and there is the Philadelphia of the Phillies baseball fans, a rowdy, exuberant, unkempt group, to say the least. In architecture, we have the Philadelphia of Paul Cret and Frank Furness, the French classicist versus the lavish freestyle medievalist. And we also have the Philadelphia of Lou Kahn and Robert Venturi. In a sense, Kahn is to Cret what Venturi is to Furness. Schlesinger's work is much more indebted to Kahn than Venturi, but one can detect a trace of Furness in his architectural personality. As is the case with any great architect, Kahn drew to himself and the school of architecture at the University of Pennsylvania many talented and productive architects and teachers. It became

known as the "Philadelphia School," and included, in addition to

Venturi, people like Romaldo Giurgola, Tim Vreeland (Schlesinger's partner for a time), John Bower, David Crane, Ian McCarg, Robert Geddes, George Qualls, and the engineer Robert le Ricolet, among others.

In the 1960's, Schlesinger both taught at Penn and worked in Kahn's studio and he fondly remembers that period as a life shaping experience. The two major projects that he worked on—undoubtedly the two most important projects of Kahns's middle period—were the Richards Medical Research Labs at Penn, and the Rochester, NY, Unitarian Church. These were buildings that put weight and substance back into architecture without the hyper-plasticity and coarseness of Brutalism and the "bunker" style of the sixties and helped American architects rediscover history as something more then historical motifs and styles. In this regard, Schlesinger judges the bathhouse at the Trenton Jewish Community Center (1955) to be Kahn's seminal building. In his view, its influence was akin to that of Mies's Farnsworth House (1950) or Rietveld's Schroeder House (1924) in that it turned heads and made people rethink their formal, constructive and aesthetic values.

As if to confirm the aesthetic side of Kahn's influence, Schlesinger went to Europe as a Harvard Wheelwright Fellow in 1963, and in Italy was much taken by two buildings: Bruneslleschi's church of Santo Spirito in Florence and the monastery of Sant'Ambrogio in Milan. Like Cret and Kahn, Brunelleschi had been an architect on the cusp of change. He was the last of the medieval master builders and the first of the Renaissance architects, and the elegance of the structural and

constructive solution, as evidenced by Santo Spirito, was important to Brunelleschi as it would be for Kahn and later
Schlesinger. Sant'Ambrogio, with its almost relentless brick-
work and its atrium courtyard also clearly made a lasting
impression on Schlesinger. There are paltry few good courtyards in the architecture of the 20th century, and as we see in
this monograph, Schlesinger has built some of them.

But, influences do not by themselves account for results.
Schlesinger has designed many courtyards, but they do not
resemble the atrium at Sant'Ambrogio. He uses brick and wood,
but not quite like Kahn. His buildings display the clarity of plan
organization, simplicity of volume, and a sensitivity to site that
his precedents evince, but are in a style unlike any of them.

Hence, it is fair to say that Schlesinger's buildings are to
architecture what Forster explains above is the novel's relation
to literature: construction, function and structure of course, but
beyond that, the aspiration to become expressive, elegant and
meaningful architecture as a result. How a building goes together is how it is configured. As Le Corbusier explained:

> "You employ stone, wood and concrete, and with
> these materials you build houses and palaces.
> That is construction. Ingenuity is at work. But
> suddenly you touch my heart, you do me good, I
> am quite happy and I say: 'This is beautiful.'
> That is Architecture. Art Enters in."

*Thomas L. Schumacher is a professor of architecture in the
School of Architecture at the University of Maryland, College
Park.*

INSTITUTIONAL

WHITEFRIARS HALL I

WASHINGTON, DC

PROJECT 1986

The original 13th century settlement of hermits on Mount Carmel in Palestine consisted of a small chapel surrounded by the individual caves of the hermits. It has been described in a history of the Carmelites as "....an oratory in the midst of the cells".

This architectural order became the basis for the form of the proposed addition to Whitefriars Hall, a Carmelite friary built in 1940 in Washington, D.C. The new bedrooms (cells) are organized around a courtyard in which the chapel (oratory) is placed.

The bedrooms follow the slope of the site and are reached by a series of stairs from the courtyard level cloister. The centrally located chapel overlooks a small garden containing a free-standing cross. On either side of the chapel's peaked central area, high clerestories bring indirect light to the spaces.

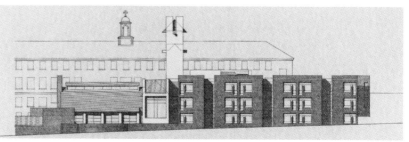

ELEVATION

WHITEFRIARS HALL II
WASHINGTON, DC
1990

A smaller version of Whitefriars I, this addition consists of a new chapel, dining room and living room arranged around a cloister that creates a perceivable and useable private outdoor space as the central element organizing the entire complex.

As in Whitefriars I, the chapel overlooks a small, raised garden containing a free-standing cross. It is developed from a cube that has two of its corners clipped off, rotating its axis 45 degrees. The remaining two corners rise to their full height, terminating this axis and providing concealed clerestories at either side of the main, peaked ceiling space that appears to float between them.

The dining room is located at the lower level of the sloping site. Entered at the upper level in the attic-like zone of the exposed wood trusses that frame the space and support a continuous monitor at the ridge of the roof, it opens to a bosque of fruit trees to the east and a terrace and amphitheater to the west. It is serviced by a kitchen and storage area located under the chapel.

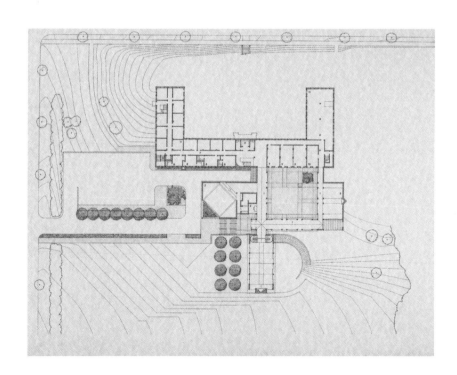

To accommodate the required program on a restricted site adjoining an existing parish church, bedroom facilities are organized in an L-shaped configuration on three upper levels while common rooms are organized at ground level. The chapel and refectory are located beyond the volume of the bedrooms, enabling them to be developed more fully in section as befits their role as the formal gathering spaces of the friary. Pulling them to the perimeter of the buildable site area also allows a traditional cloister to be developed as the central element organizing the complex.

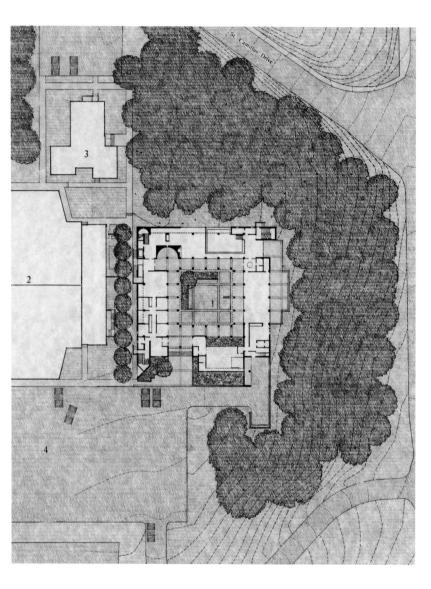

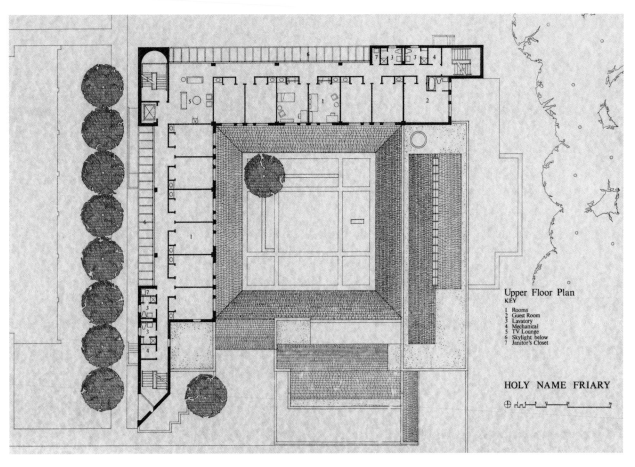

Upper Floor Plan
KEY

1 Rooms
2 Guest Room
3 Lavatory
4 Mechanical
5 TV Lounge
6 Skylight below
7 Janitor's Closet

HOLY NAME FRIARY

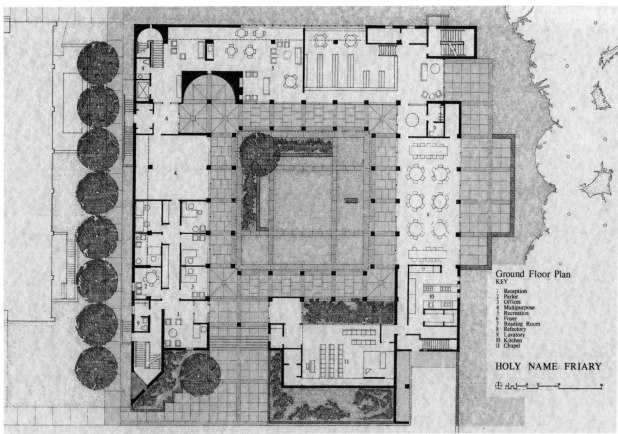

Ground Floor Plan
KEY

1 Reception
2 Parlor
3 Offices
4 Multipurpose
5 Recreation
6 Foyer
7 Reading Room
8 Refectory
9 Lavatory
10 Kitchen
11 Chapel

HOLY NAME FRIARY

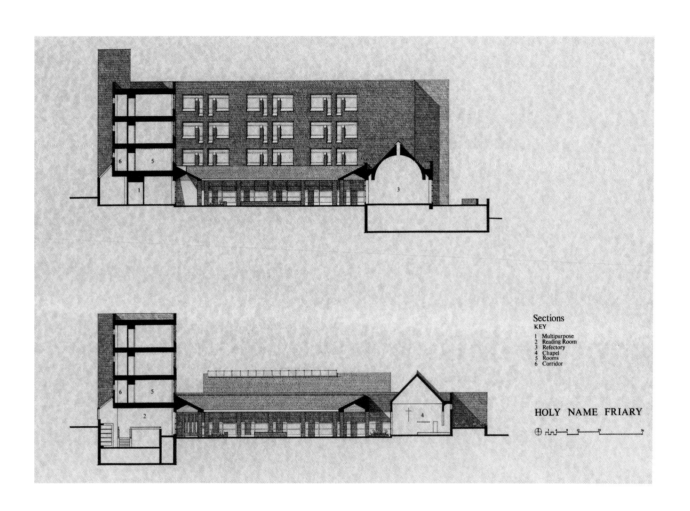

Sections
KEY

1 Multipurpose
2 Reading Room
3 Refectory
4 Chapel
5 Rooms
6 Corridor

HOLY NAME FRIARY

ST. MARY'S AT THE CATHEDRAL
EPISCOPAL DIOCESE OF PHILADELPHIA
PHILADELPHIA, PA
PROJECT 1970

During the depression the Episcopal Diocese was forced to postpone plans for the construction of a major cathedral. Since that time the local parish has been "temporarily" quartered in the only portion of the cathedral that had actually been constructed, the ambulatory Mother Chapel. Finally, the Diocese abandoned all hope of completing the cathedral and this study was done to explore the feasibility of providing a permanent home for the local parish.

The solution proposes a new church structure that is separated from the original chapel by an atrium, the only physical connection being at the entry point. The old and the new will then reinforce each other visually while providing historical continuity. The separation of structures also allows a staging program that will not result in a loss of the congregation during construction.

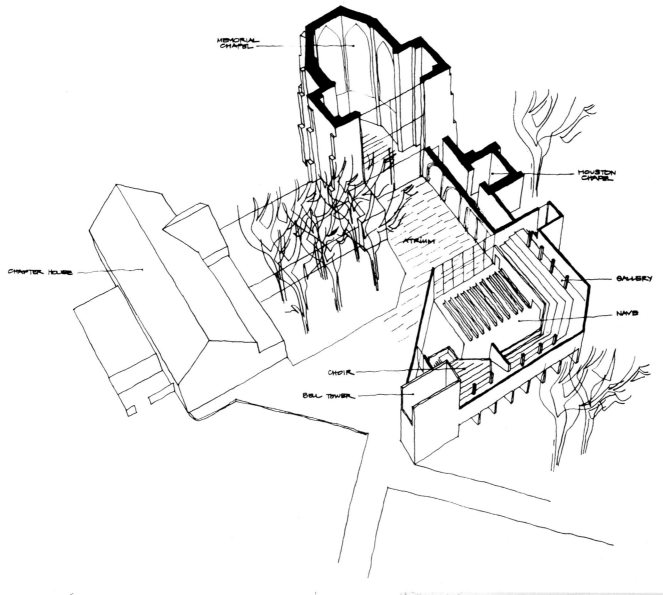

MEMORIAL CHAPEL

HOUSTON CHAPEL

CHAPTER HOUSE

ATRIUM

GALLERY

NAVE

CHOIR

BELL TOWER

COMMERCIAL

NATIONAL PLACE
WASHINGTON, DC
1981

This building, at the corner of 14th and F Streets, is the office, retail, and parking component of a mixed use project in downtown Washington. The fourth component is a hotel at 13th Street and Pennsylvania Avenue designed by Mitchell Giurgola Associates. In section, eleven levels, contain 400,000 square feet of office space are located above a three-level, 100,000 square-foot retail mall. The lower retail level is connected to the hotel lobby by a shopping concourse. Below the retail are four levels of parking accommodating 400 cars.

The office floors are broken into two wings in order to minimize distance to exterior windows as well as create a courtyard that allows the lower retail to be skylite. The elevator core is located between these two wings allowing the elevator lobby to overlook the courtyard as well.

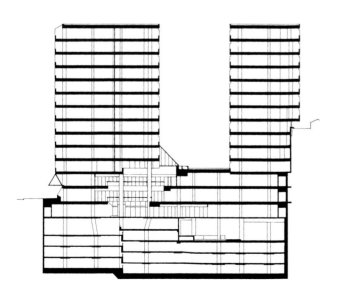

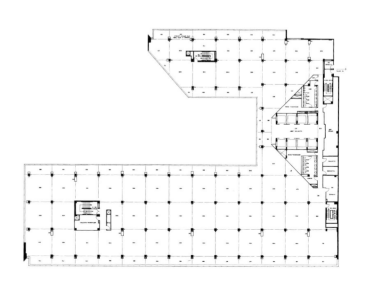

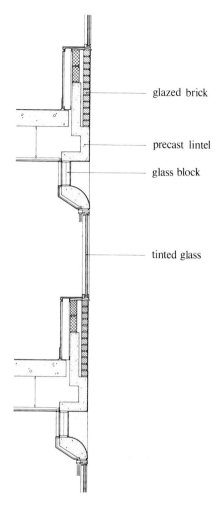

glazed brick

precast lintel

glass block

tinted glass

NATIONAL PLACE

RESTAURANTS/CAFES/FOOD SHOPS
American Cafe
Au Bon Pain
Bagel Place
Bull on the Beach
Everything Yogurt
Haagen-Dazs
Hershey's Cookies
Hershey's Chocolate Memories
House of Almonds
Hunan Express
Incredible Vegetable
Corn Crib

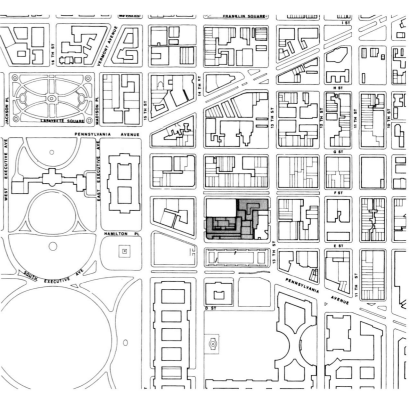

1301 PENNSYLVANIA AVENUE
WASHINGTON, DC
1979

The formal intent of the building was to present a restrained and dignified façade facing L'Enfant's restored Western Plaza, while allowing a more exuberant development of the building as it turns the corner and works its way up the slope of 13th Street to the retail activity on F Street.

The first two floors accommodate lobbies and retail space interconnected by a public concourse. The upper ten floors contain 195,000 square feet of rental space. All elevators open onto double-height elevator lobbies allowing natural light and exterior views.

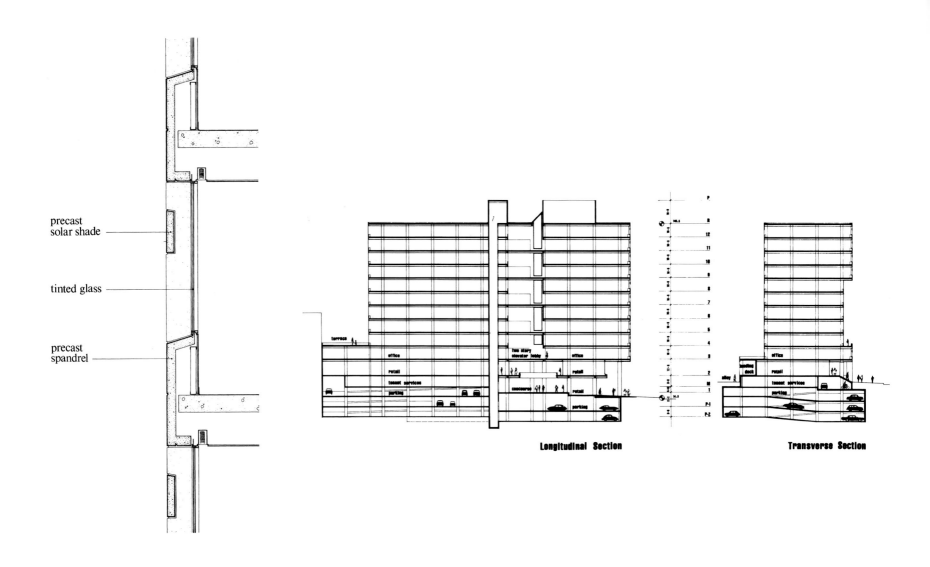

precast
solar shade

tinted glass

precast
spandrel

Longitudinal Section

Transverse Section

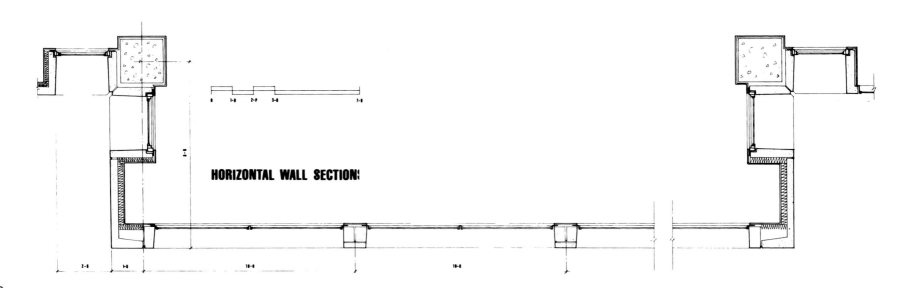

HORIZONTAL WALL SECTIONS

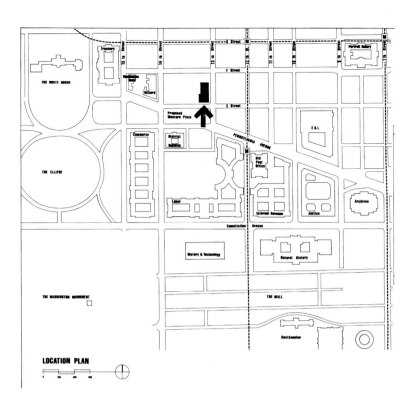

LOCATION PLAN

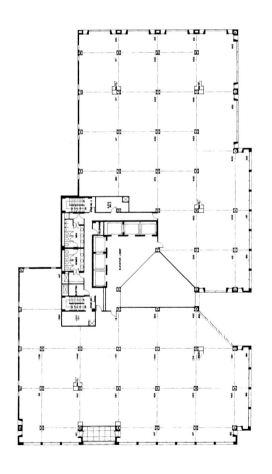

PRESIDENTIAL BUILDING ADDITION
WASHINGTON, D.C.
PROJECT 1989

T he site of this proposed addition is an air-right slot of space, 40 feet wide by 100 feet deep, located over the garage entrance to the existing Presidential office building on Pennsylvania Avenue. The addition attempts to maintain its own perceivable architectural presence in this urban setting by acting as a visual pause between the divergent rhythms and styles of the Evening Star building to its left and the Hotel Harrington to its right.

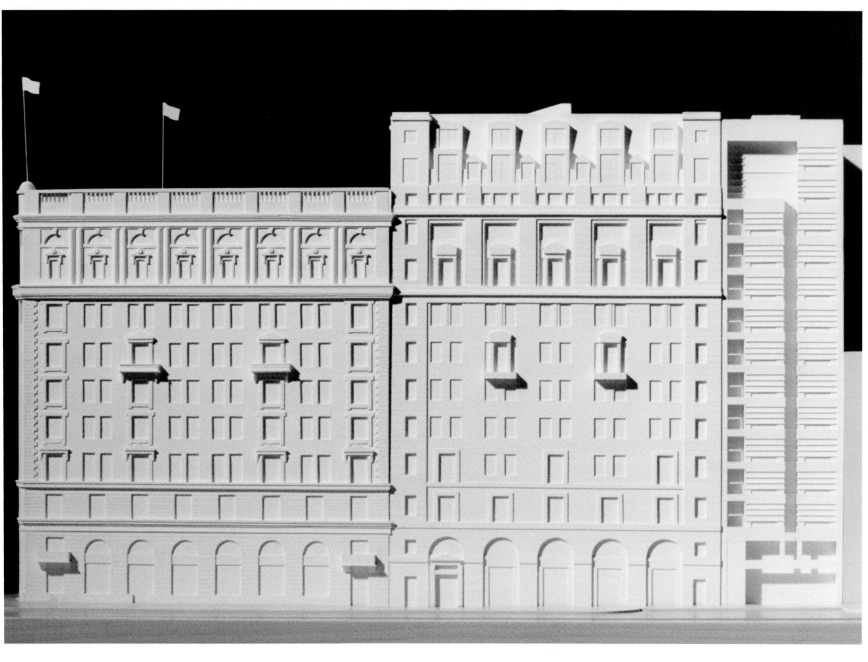

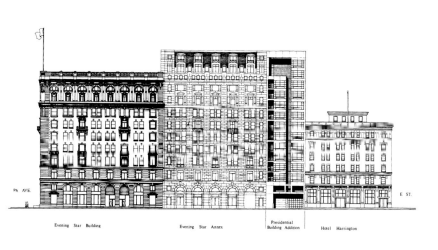

Evening Star Building   Evening Star Annex   Presidential
                                                           Building Addition   Hotel Harrington

PA. AVE.   E. ST.

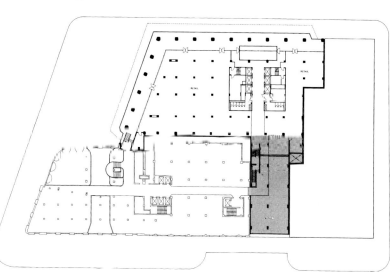

PROTOTYPE SERVICE STATION
GULF OIL CORPORATION
PROJECT 1968

T he major design element is a three-sided, 24-foot-high, brick wall, which acts to provide enough bulk and height to "hold" a corner location and avoid the usual open sea of asphalt. It also screens the usual service station clutter of outdoor sales, vending machines, tire storage and rest rooms while consolidating, in one architectural feature, signage with a maximum of identity.

SECTION

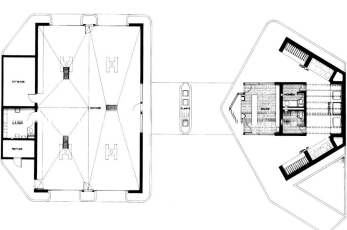

EDUCATIONAL

ST. FRANCIS OF ASSISI PARISH SCHOOL
TRIANGLE, VIRGINIA
2001

I n addition to classroom and office space, this 28,000-square-foot addition to an existing classroom wing provided much needed support facilities, including a library, gymnasium and cafeteria, that were lacking in the original 1950 facility.

An important design goal was the introduction of natural light into the major rooms and circulation areas. This was achieved through the deployment of skylights and internal courtyards throughout the building.

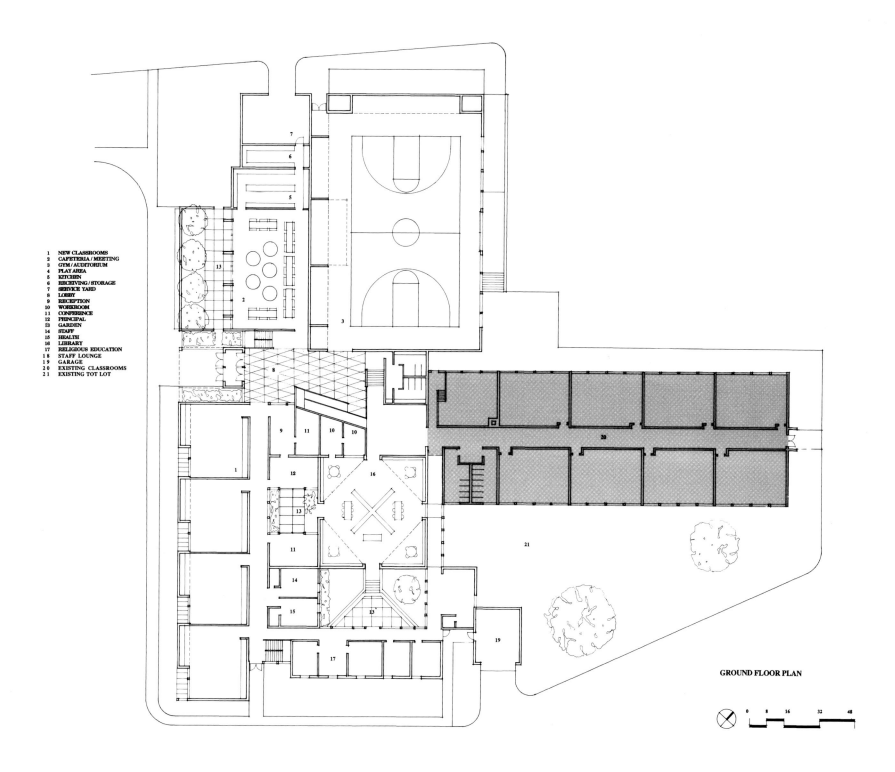

1 NEW CLASSROOMS
2 CAFETERIA / MEETING
3 GYM / AUDITORIUM
4 PLAY AREA
5 KITCHEN
6 RECEIVING / STORAGE
7 SERVICE YARD
8 LOBBY
9 RECEPTION
10 WORKROOM
11 CONFERENCE
12 PRINCIPAL
13 GARDEN
14 STAFF
15 HEALTH
16 LIBRARY
17 RELIGIOUS EDUCATION
18 STAFF LOUNGE
19 GARAGE
20 EXISTING CLASSROOMS
21 EXISTING TOT LOT

GROUND FLOOR PLAN

0 8 16   32   48

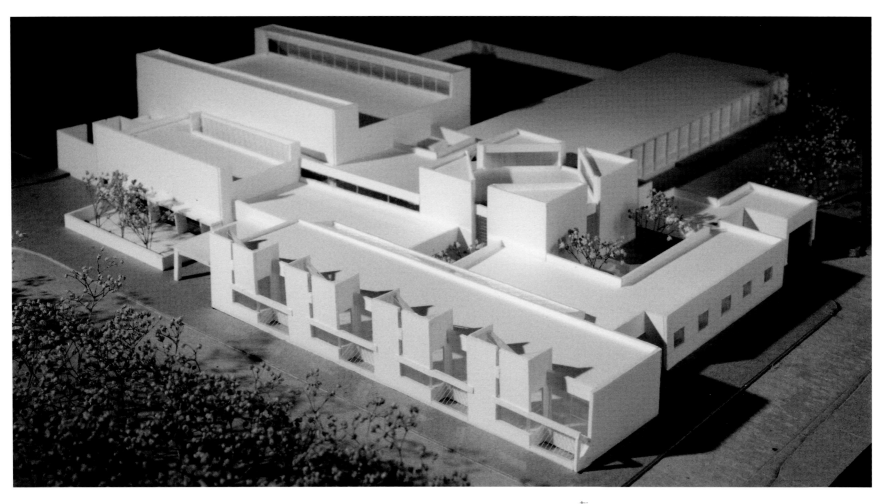

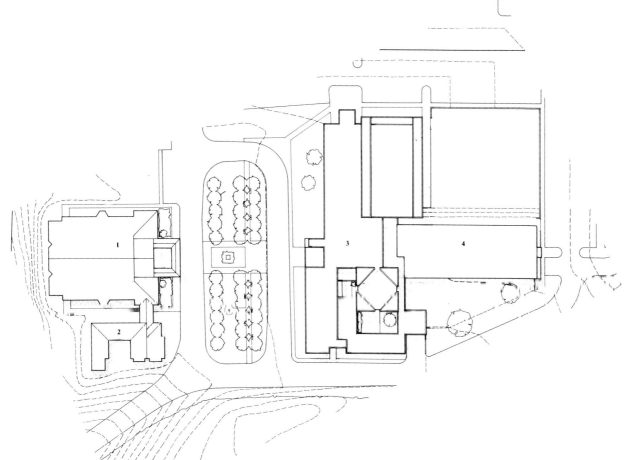

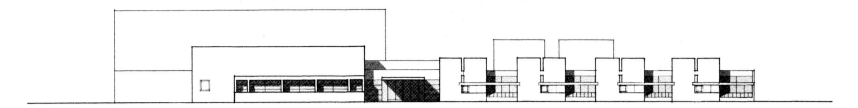

SOUTHWEST ELEVATION

NATIONAL CATHEDRAL SCHOOL
WASHINGTON, DC
2000

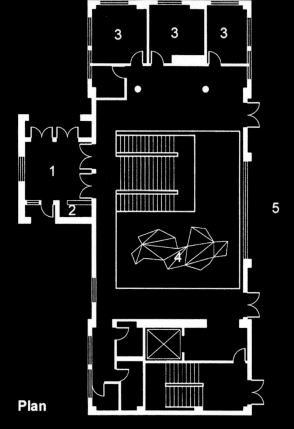

Plan

1. Entry Foyer
2. Contol Desk
3. Staff Offices
4. Climbing Wall
5. Playing Fields
6. Gym
7. Lockers

I n order to avoid constructing a large field house on grounds adjoining a residential neighborhood, the National Cathedral School elected to build an underground facility that accommodates three practice gyms, a competition gym, training rooms, weight rooms and locker rooms, all located under a full size, on-grade soccer field constructed on the facilities roof.

This project is the "Headhouse" of that facility. It acts as its' on-grade entrance and connects to the lower levels by way of a three story atrium that is organized around a free standing "climbing wall" and stairs that descend to the gym level. Athletic staff offices are located at the upper level overlooking the soccer field.

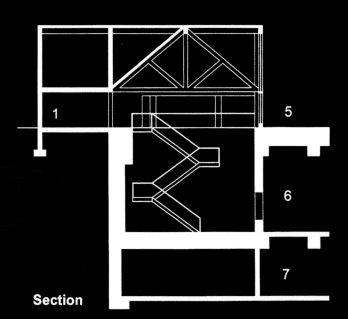

Section

RESEARCH LABORATORY
UNIVERSITY OF PENNSYLVANIA
PHILADELPHIA, PA
1964
IN ASSOCIATION WITH T.R. VREELAND

This is a second floor addition to a one story greenhouse service building designed by Louis Kahn. The "key-hole" window reflects the existing fenestration on the first floor but the proportions and rhythm are changed to serve a different set of interior conditions. The vertical element becomes a narrow view slit to provide a maximum of laboratory wall space while the horizontal element is raised above the beam line to form a clerestory and service chase monitor. By feeding services down from this monitor rather than up from the lower level, innumerable penetrations of the existing 8-inch slab were avoided and ease and flexibility for future change maintained.

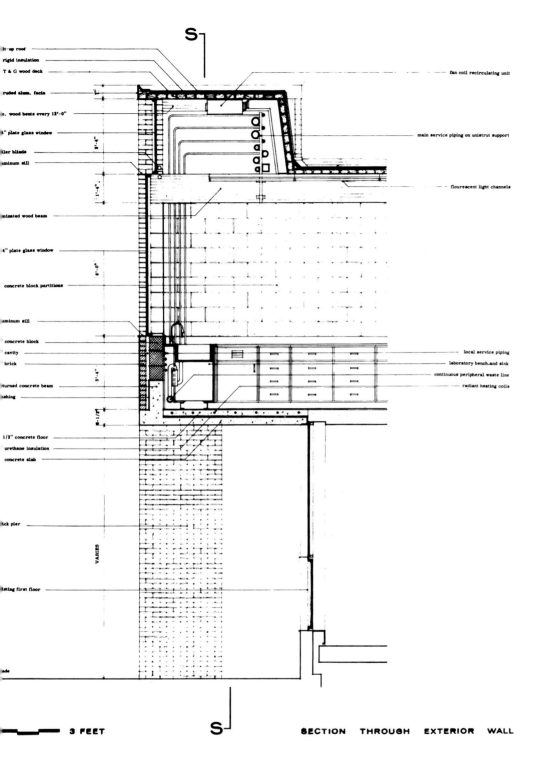

lt-up roof
rigid insulation
T & G wood deck
ruded alum. facia
n. wood beams every 12'-0"
3" plate glass window
ler blinds
minum sill

minated wood beam

4" plate glass window

concrete block partitions

minum sill

concrete block
cavity
brick

turned concrete beam
ashing

1/2" concrete floor
urethane insulation
concrete slab

ick pier

VARIES

isting first floor

ade

fan coil recirculating unit

main service piping on unistrut support

flourescent light channels

local service piping
laboratory bench and sink
continuous peripheral waste line
radiant heating coils

3 FEET   S   SECTION THROUGH EXTERIOR WALL

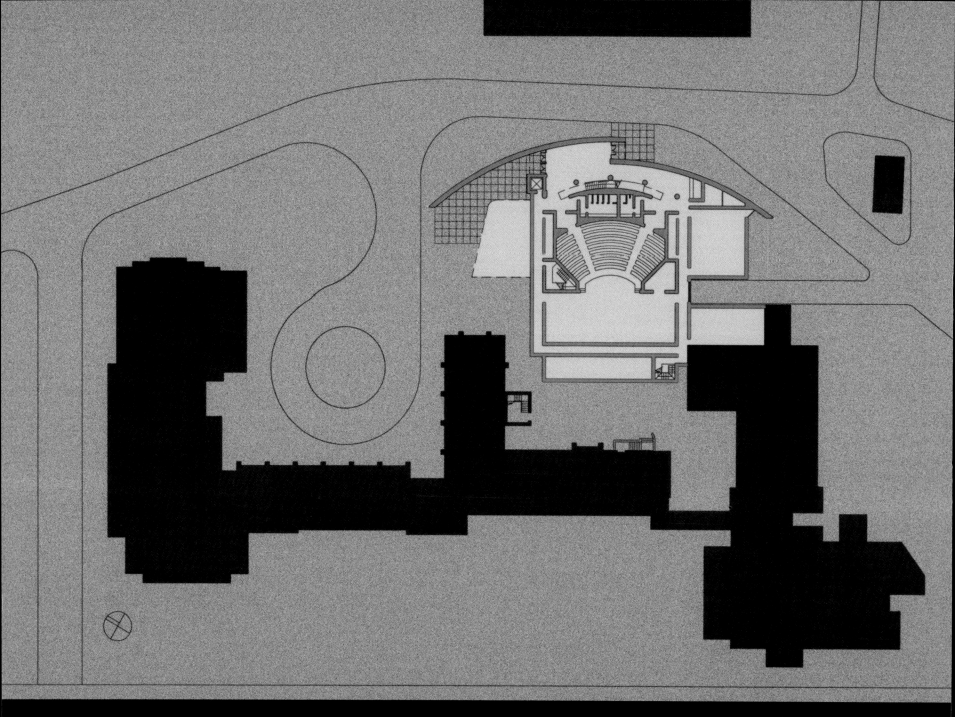

PERFORMING ARTS CENTER
STONE RIDGE SCHOOL
BETHESDA, MARYLAND
PROJECT 2003

Over a period of many decades, the academic buildings of the Stone Ridge School have developed as a series of interconnected additions—the latest will be this 20,000 square foot performing arts center, which will provide facilities for music, dance and drama programs. In addition to teaching studios and classrooms, there will be a 378-seat theater, dressing rooms, offices and a small music library.

The expansive curved entrance façade is meant to screen and unify the diverse rear façades of the existing academic wings and will be centered on the school's other main public venue, the existing gymnasium across the access driveway.

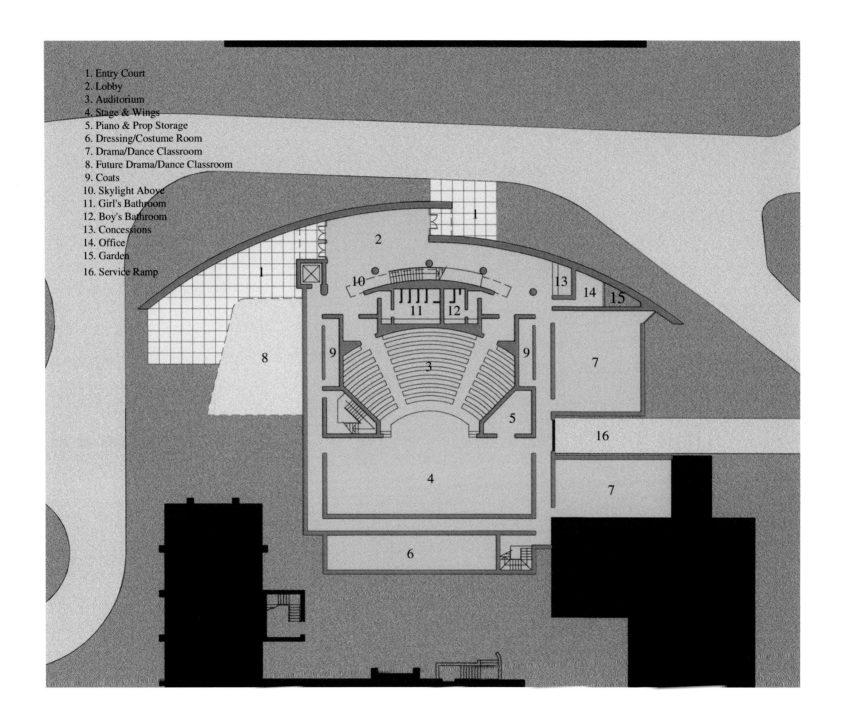

1. Entry Court
2. Lobby
3. Auditorium
4. Stage & Wings
5. Piano & Prop Storage
6. Dressing/Costume Room
7. Drama/Dance Classroom
8. Future Drama/Dance Classroom
9. Coats
10. Skylight Above
11. Girl's Bathroom
12. Boy's Bathroom
13. Concessions
14. Office
15. Garden
16. Service Ramp

On an extremely tight and complex urban setting, this addition will provide new classrooms for middle school students as well as new facilities for art, drama and an expanded library. The library, a skylit court-yard, is intended to act as the unifying heart of both the middle and upper schools.

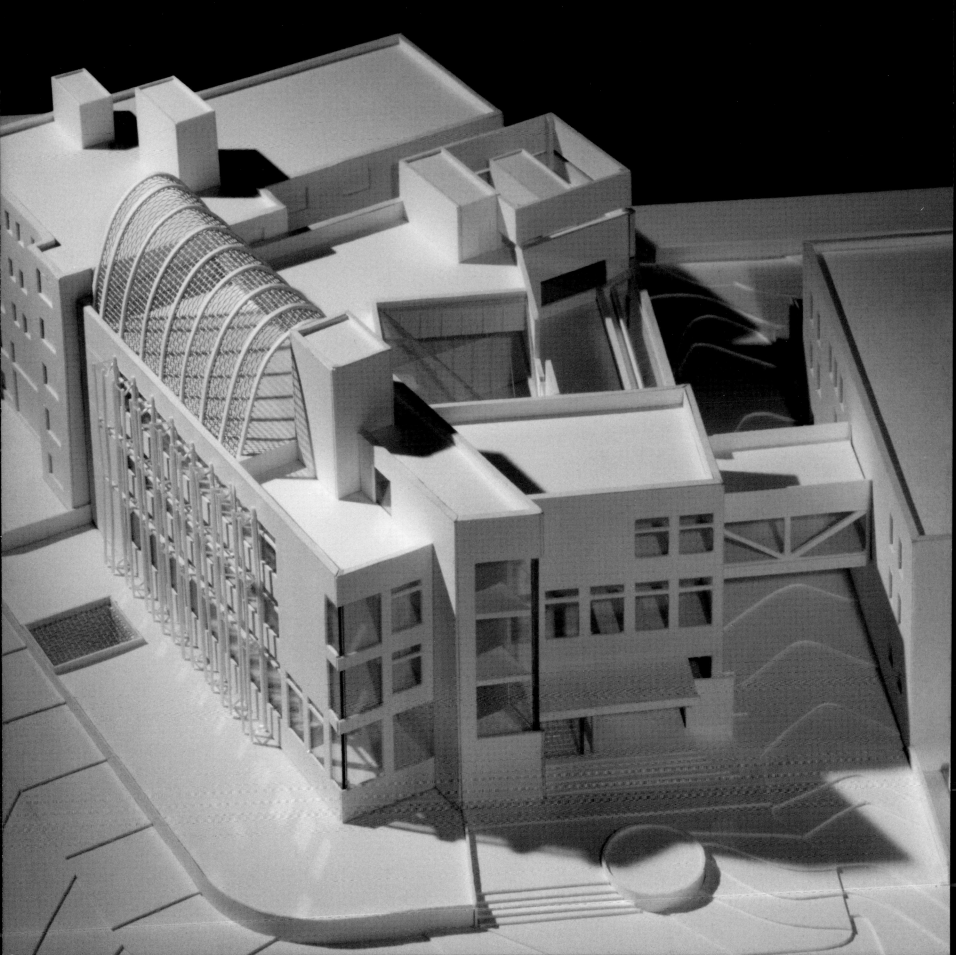

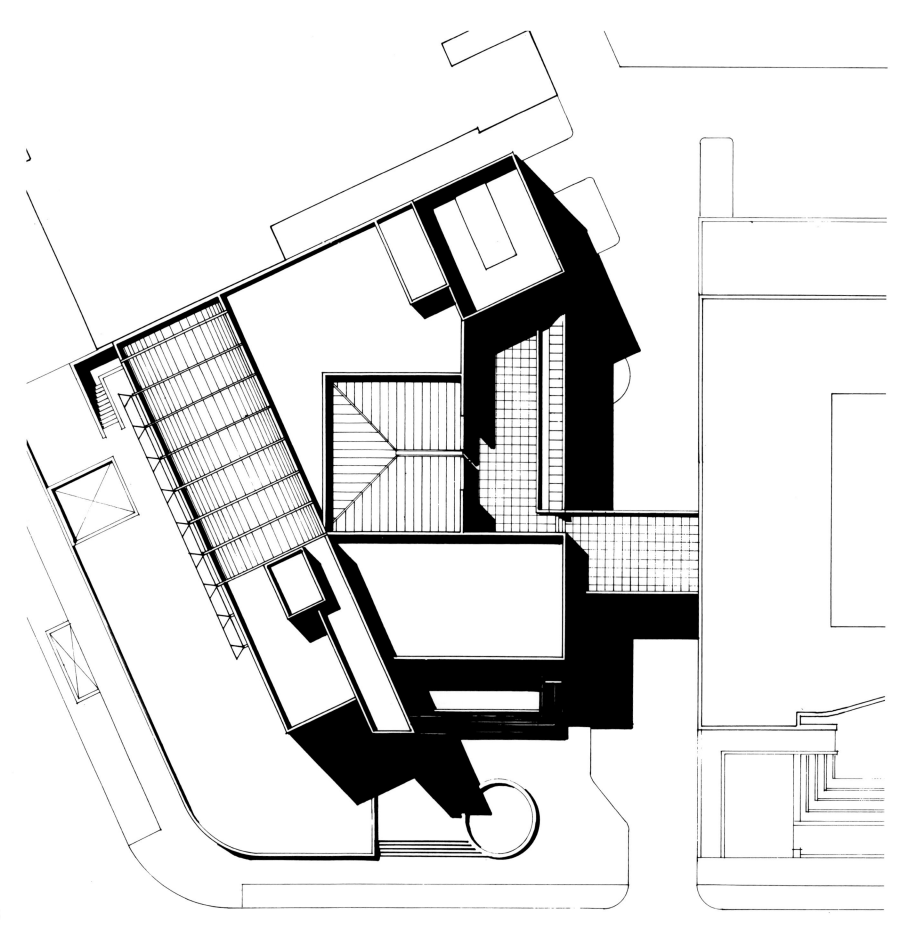

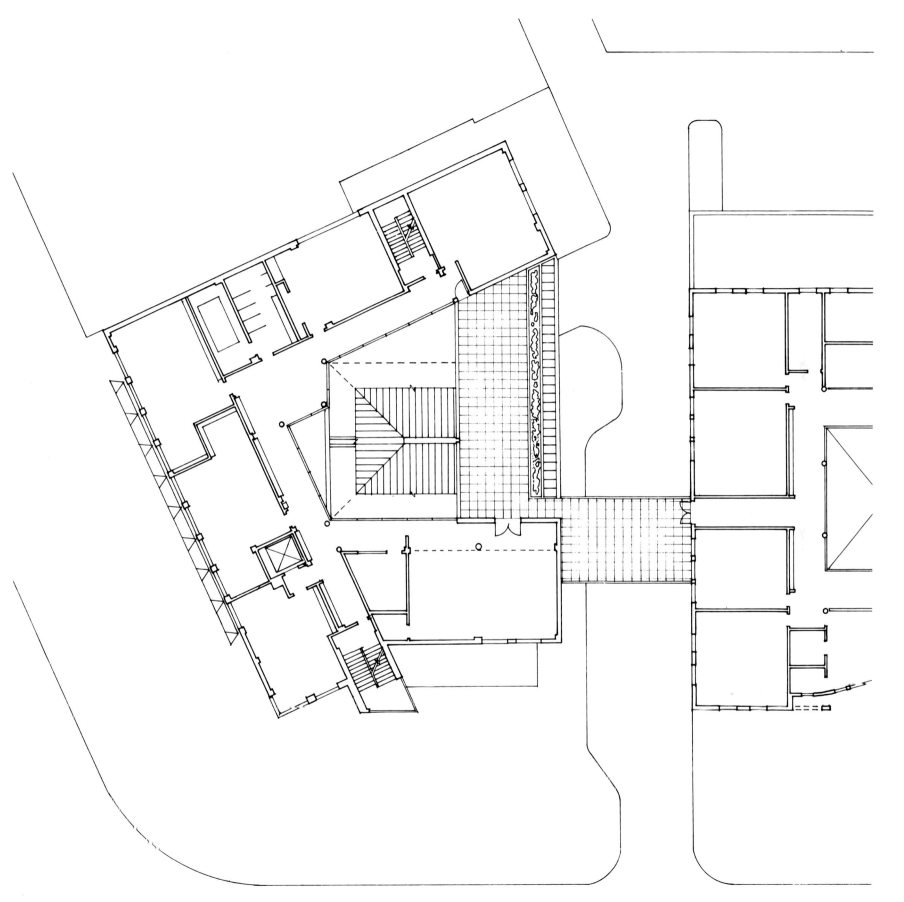

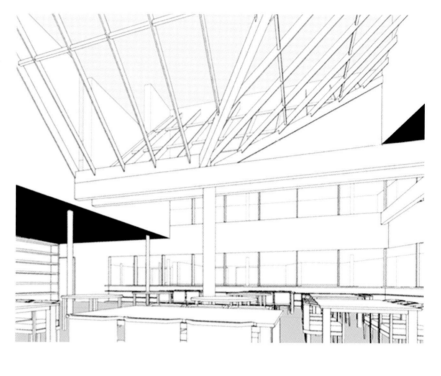

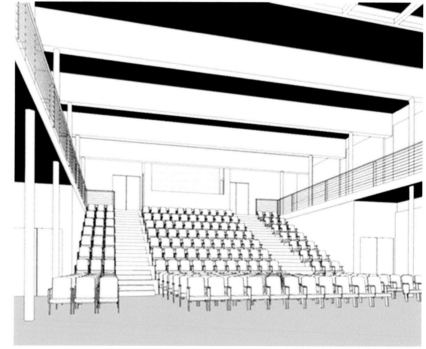

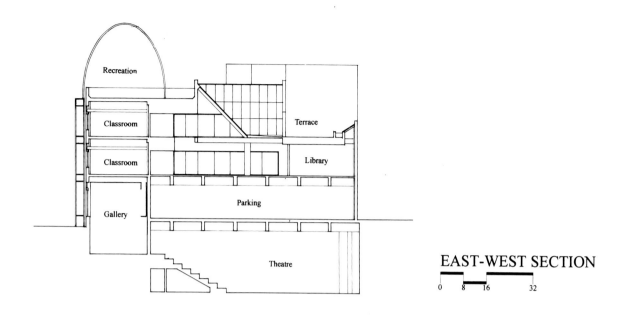

EAST-WEST SECTION

0   8   16   32

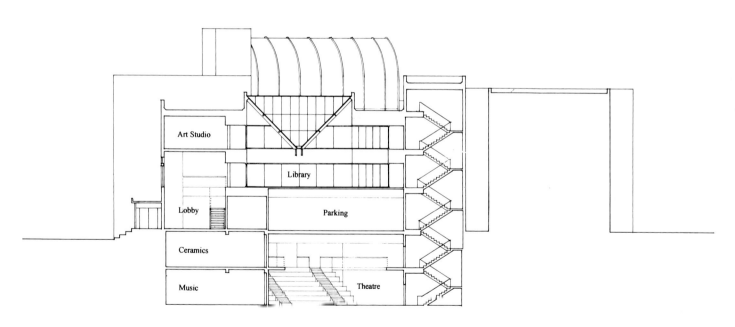

NORTH SOUTH SECTION

0   8   16   32

FINE ARTS CENTER
ST. BONAVENTURE UNIVERSITY

Besides providing art galleries, studios and a recital hall in the heart of the academic core, this facility will contribute to the overall image of the campus by completing and reinforcing an important corner of the college commons, replace a nondescript, one storey post office building whose presence is inappropriate in this important location, and screen the campus steam plant and service area from public view.

EXISTING

PROPOSED

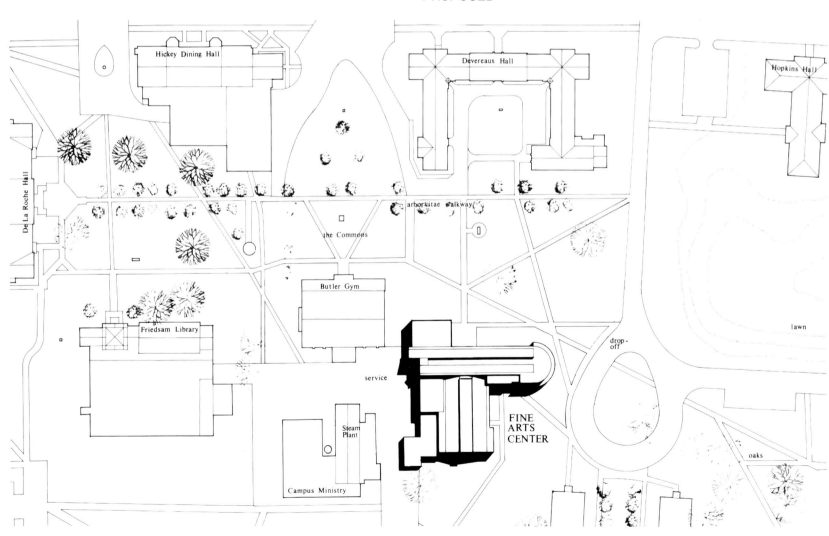

80

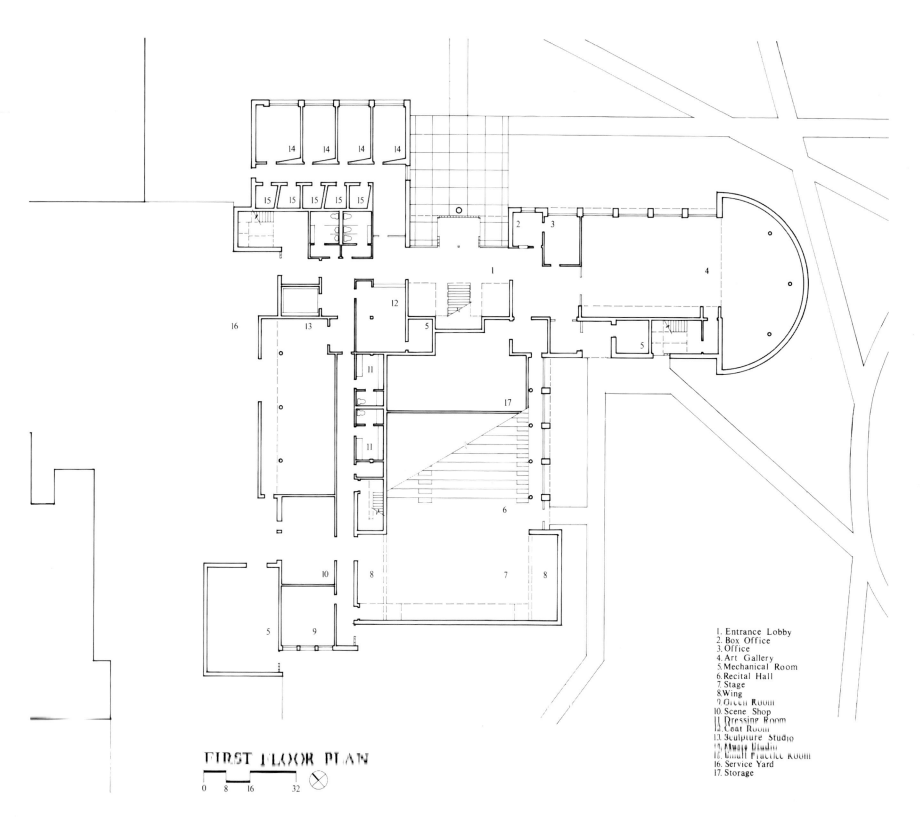

FIRST FLOOR PLAN

0   8   16   32   ⊗

1. Entrance Lobby
2. Box Office
3. Office
4. Art Gallery
5. Mechanical Room
6. Recital Hall
7. Stage
8. Wing
9. Green Room
10. Scene Shop
11. Dressing Room
12. Coat Room
13. Sculpture Studio
14. Music Studio
15. Small Practice Room
16. Service Yard
17. Storage

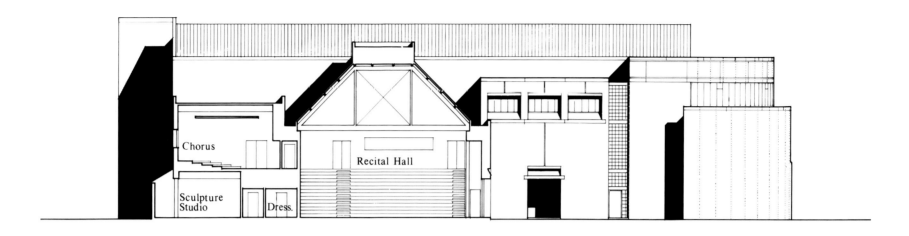

EAST-WEST SECTION

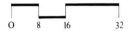

O 8 16 32

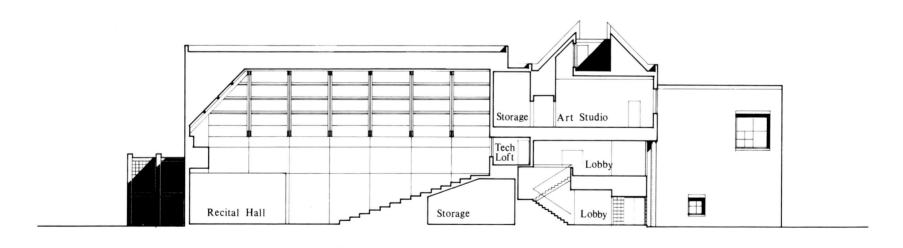

NORTH-SOUTH SECTION

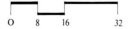

O 8 16 32

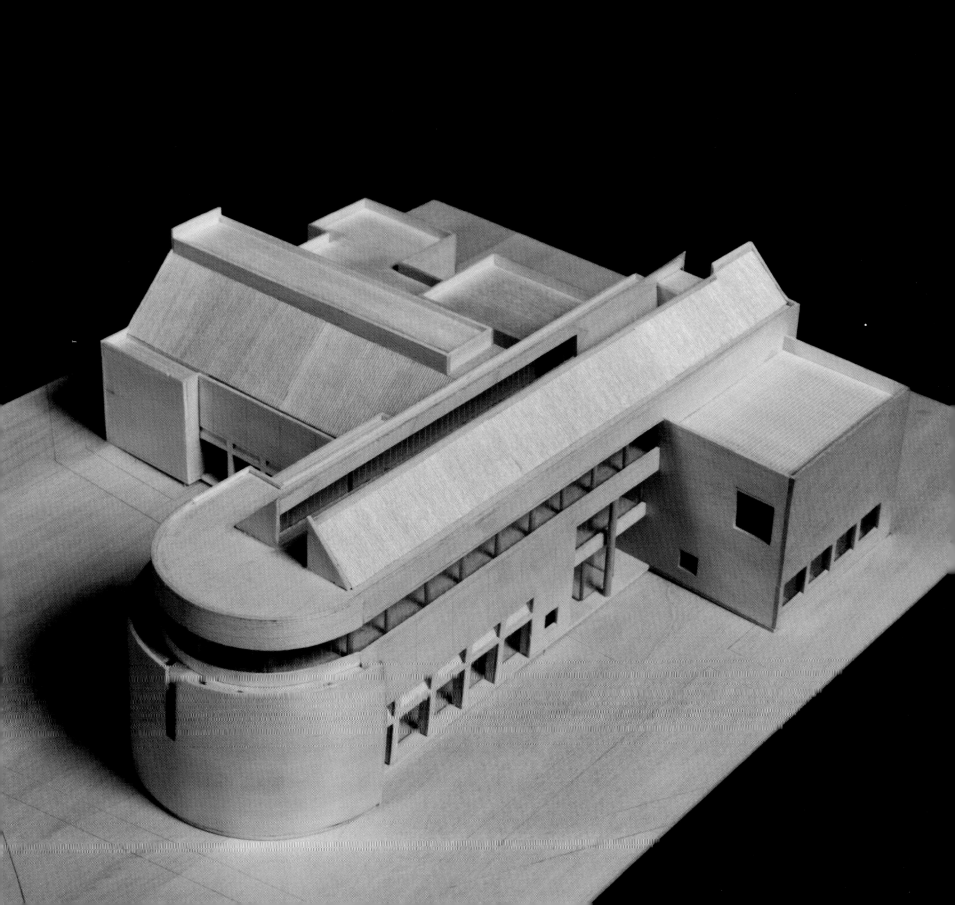

MIXED-USE

T his project, part of a total block development by EastBanc, Inc. known as Design Center West, is located in the waterfront district of Georgetown in Washington, D.C. on the site of an abandoned, one story building fronting on the C & O canal. The apartment is a rental unit located over new, first floor retail space.

The site is zoned "W-1 Waterfront District". This zoning limited any use, other than residential, to an FAR of 1. This allowable FAR of 3,630 square feet was utilized for the retail space on the first floor. The apartment on the second floor was limited by zoning to 80 percent coverage, resulting in an apartment size of 2,900 square feet. The resulting open space requirement of 715 square feet, combined with a height restriction that limited the apartment height to one story became the design rationale for the "courtyard" parti of the unit.

The new load-bearing façade on the C & O canal is designed to suggest the site's industrial history by incorporating a pallet of brick arches, piers and walls.

BEFORE

AFTER

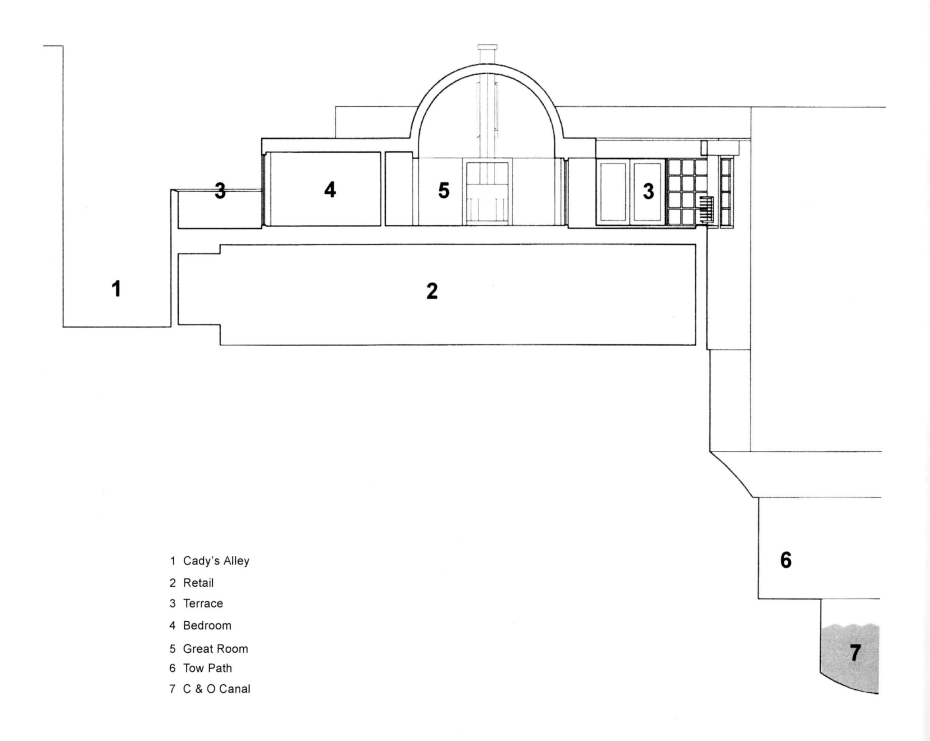

1 Cady's Alley

2 Retail

3 Terrace

4 Bedroom

5 Great Room

6 Tow Path

7 C & O Canal

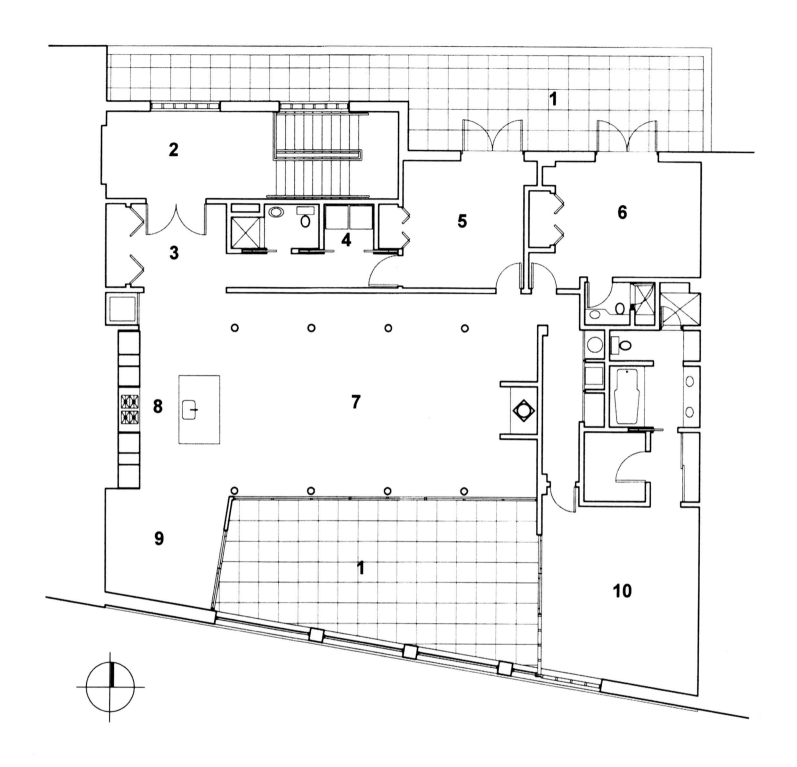

1 Terrace   5 Bedroom/ Study   8 Kitchen

2 Entry Stair   6 Bedroom   9 Dining

3 Foyer   7 Great Room   10 Master Bedrrom

4 Laundry

The sectional organization of this mixed-use building accommodates residential units on the upper floors, two middle levels of office space, and street level and basement retail facilities. Required on-grade parking is located at the rear of the site with drive-through access from the street.

A common elevator lobby serves the residential and office floors. Entrance to the four apartments—two one-bedroom flats and two two-bedroom/study duplexes—are on the fourth floor. The upper level of each duplex contains two bedrooms, a study and an interior courtyard that overlooks the two-story dining room below.

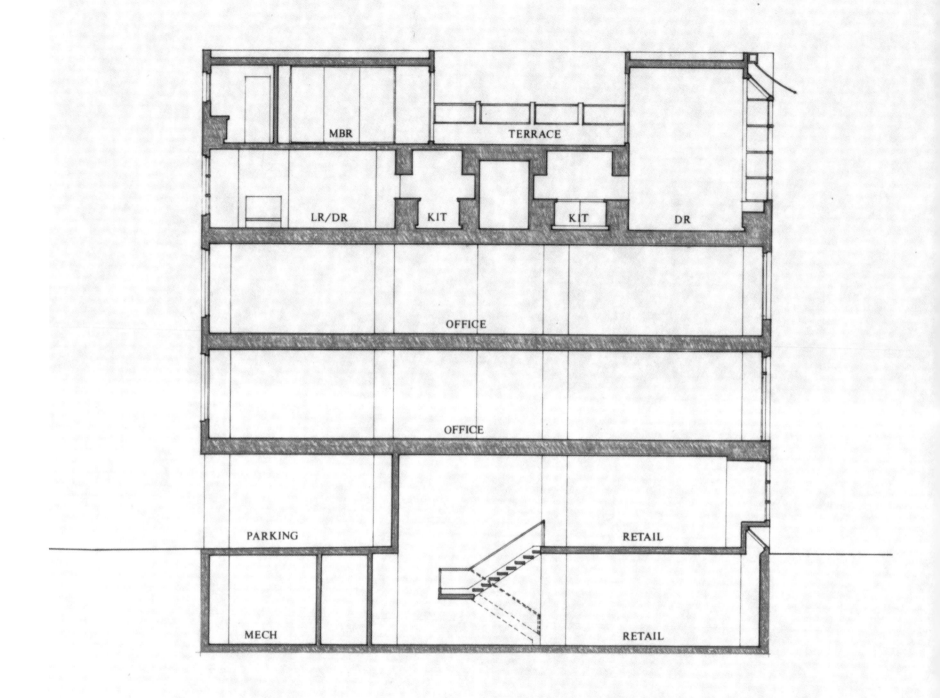

North-South Section

```
0    4    8         16
```

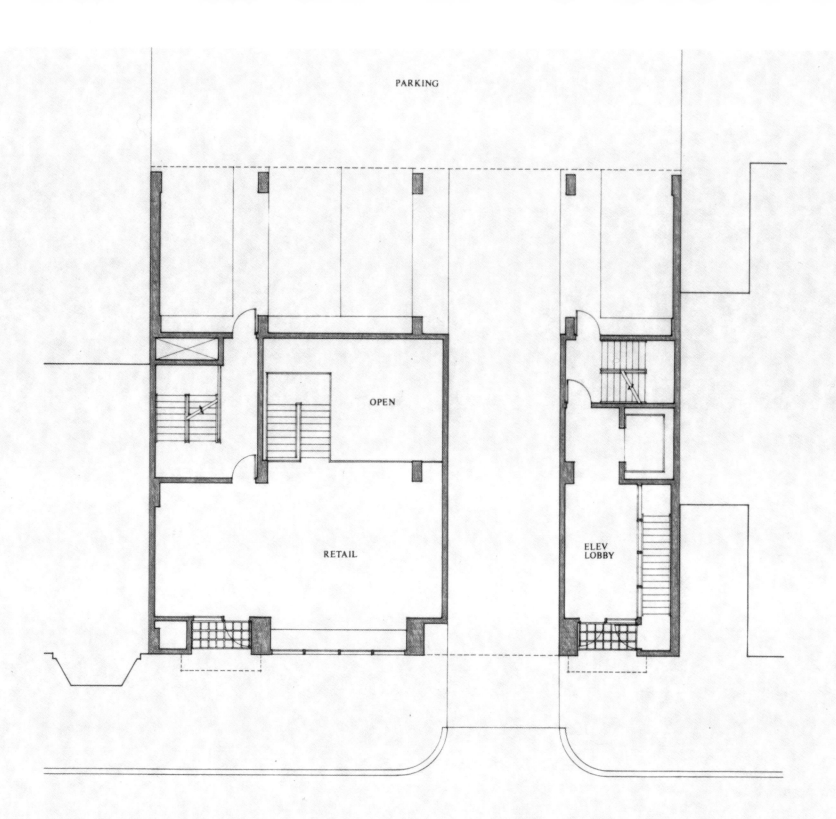

PARKING

OPEN

RETAIL

ELEV
LOBBY

First Floor Plan

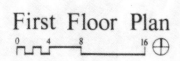

0   4   8   16

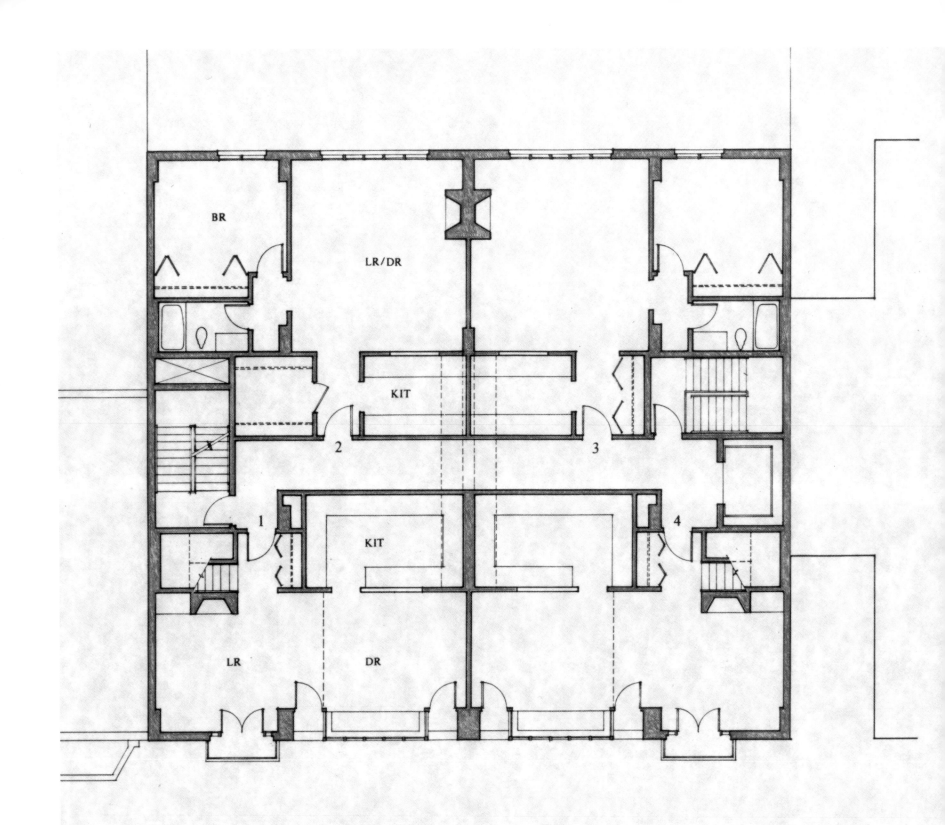

BR

LR/DR

KIT

2

3

1

4

KIT

LR

DR

Fourth Floor Plan

0   4   8   16

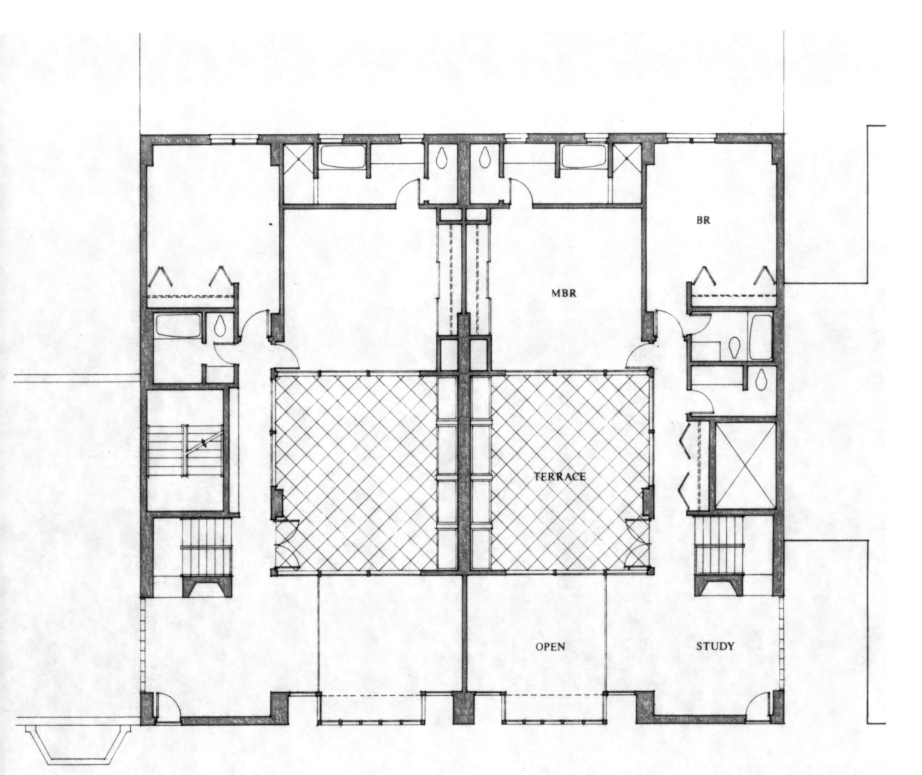

BR

MBR

TERRACE

OPEN

STUDY

Fifth Floor Plan

0 4 8 16

1810-12 WISCONSIN AVENUE
WASHINGTON, DC
PROJECT 1990

This in-fill, mixed-use building accommodates duplex residential units on the upper floors, two middle levels of office space, and retail facilities at the street and basement levels. Simple rows of French doors and "punched" window openings at the office levels serve as a foil to

the more exuberant and specific treatment of the residential and retail elevations.

The juxtaposition of the solidity of the office floors to the relative porosity of the duplex apartment levels establishes a reading of the façade that corresponds to the height of the adjoining lower buildings and also acts as a transition to an existing 3-story apartment house. Chimneys animate the skyline and emphasize the image of the residential component that terminates the façade.

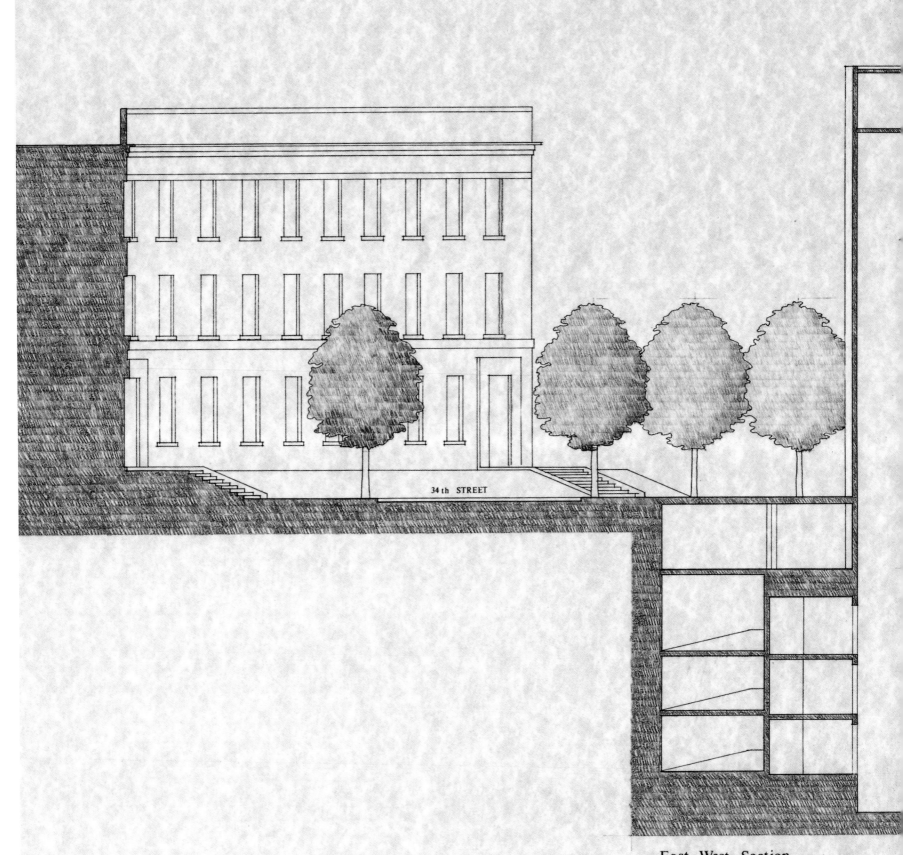

34th STREET

East - West Section

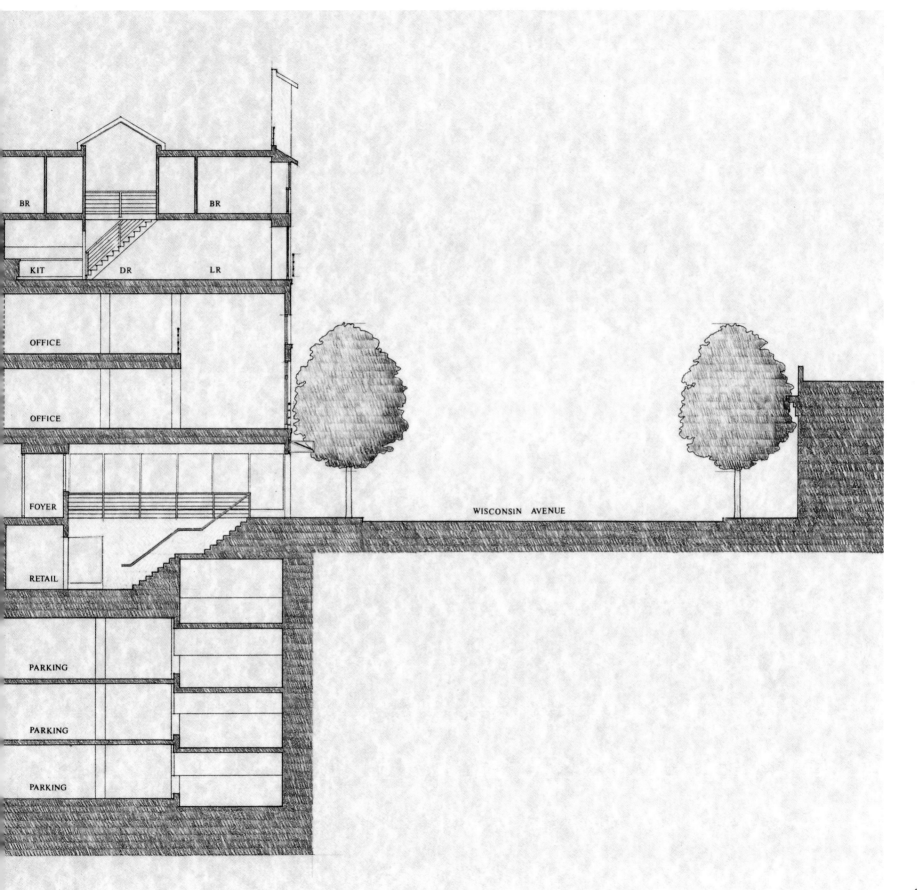

BR

BR

KIT   DR   LR

OFFICE

OFFICE

FOYER

RETAIL

PARKING

PARKING

PARKING

WISCONSIN AVENUE

The smaller apartment units are raised above masonry enclosed office suites on a laminated wood structural system. The resulting "gap" between the two structures is glazed by a continuous skylight providing private, top-lite exam rooms at the perimeter with labs, toilets and services in the core. The apartments are reached from communal decks with access to a central parking area. Office parking is at the extremity of the site and provides access to ground floor reception areas.

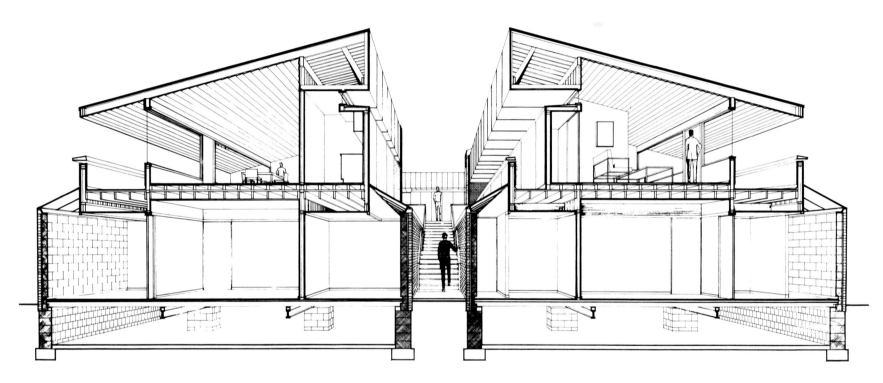

PERSPECTIVE SECTION

MULTIFAMILY

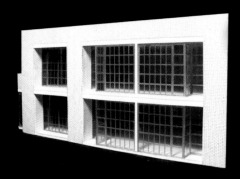

3303 WATER STREET
WASHINGTON, DC
2004
IN ASSOCIATION WITH GARY EDWARD HANDEL.

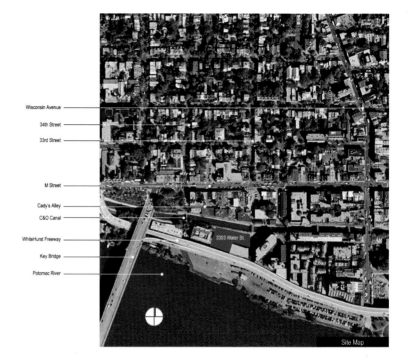

Wisconsin Avenue
34th Street
33rd Street
M Street
Cady's Alley
C&O Canal
WhiteHurst Freeway
Key Bridge
Potomac River

3303 Water St.

Site Map

The project, developed by EastBanc, Inc., is a 72-unit condominium located on the historic C & O Canal in Washington, D.C. Because the site is not the Georgetown of Federal townhouse, but rather the Georgetown of what was the industrial waterfront, the building attempts to evoke the spirit of that era through a simple, strong vocabulary of stone pieirs and glass in-fill. The building can be thought of as an industrial mill that has been converted into a series of loft apartments designed with floor-to-ceiling windows to take advantage of the unique views the site has to offer: the canal and the cityscape of Georgetown to the north and the Potomac River to the south. At night, the same larege areas of glass cause the building to glow llike a Chinese lantern.

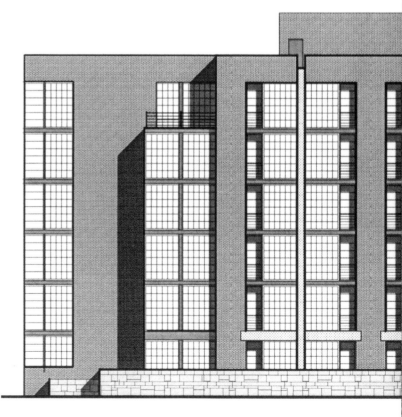

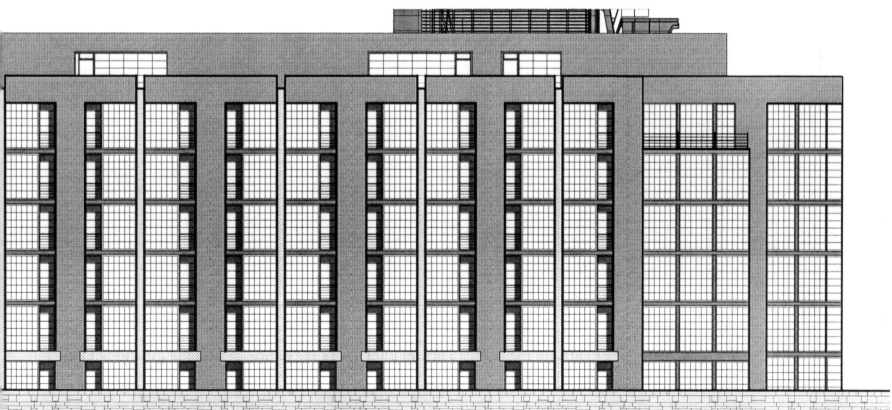

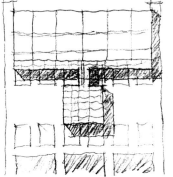

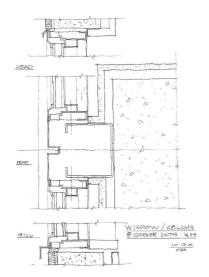

WINDOW / COLUMN
@ CORNER UNITS 1/4"=1'
10-13-01
FSA

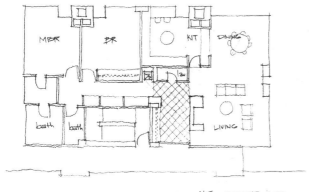

N.E. CORNER UNIT
2BR / 2 1/2 B
7/30/01
FSA

MARINE GUARD QUARTERS
PORT-AU-PRINCE, HAITI
1981

This project for the U.S. embassy in Haiti is located on a hillside overlooking Port-au-Prince. At an altitude of 100 meters above sea level, it provides magnificent views to the north, moderated temperatures and exposure to prevailing breezes. The southern portion of the three-quarter-acre site is relatively flat while the remainder drops 14 meters to the north.

The flat area of the site is utilized for vehicular access, parking, and entrance. The public and private areas of the building are located along the ridge of the site facing the view to the north and act as a buffer between the active vehicular zone and the quiet zone of bedrooms terracing down the north slope.

The entrance courtyard is defined by three pavilions: one is a "gateway" to the complex, a second is a porte-cochere, and the third accommodates servant's quarters.

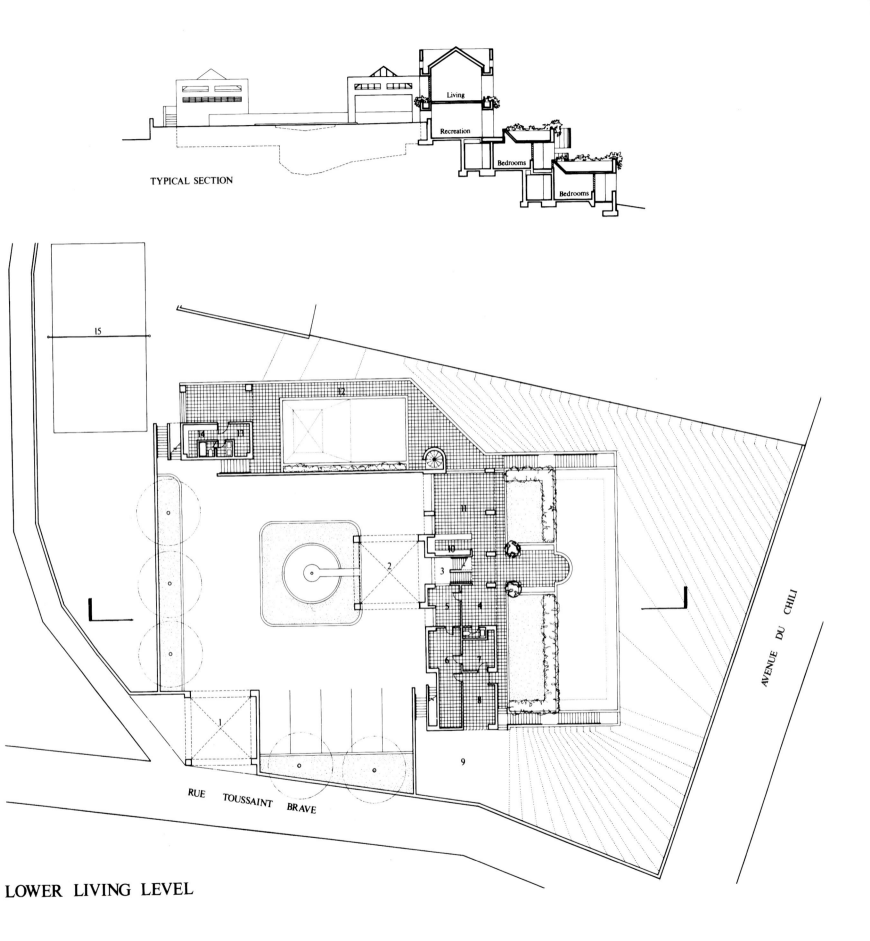

TYPICAL SECTION

Living

Recreation

Bedrooms

Bedrooms

15

14 13

12

11

10

2

3

5 4

6 7

8

1

9

RUE TOUSSAINT BRAVE

AVENUE DU CHILI

LOWER LIVING LEVEL

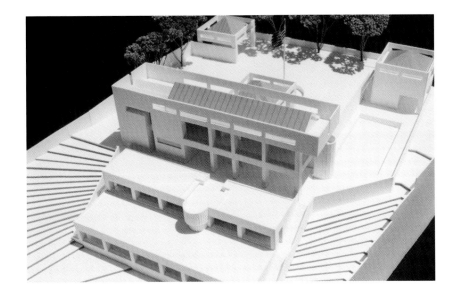

CHRISTY VILLAGE
BEACH MOUNTAIN, NC
1972

Fourteen apartments are organized as a series of seven, three story units, each containing a two bedroom and a three bedroom apartment. The level area of the site was designated for parking while the seven units are staggered in plan and stepped down at four-foot intervals to conform to the sloping site and setback lines.

The "L" shape of the units allow extensive amounts of deck area to be tucked away into the "L" for privacy. Each two and three bedroom apartment shares a common covered entry, which also accommodates storage lockers. From the entry, the two bedroom apartment is down half a flight. The three bedroom apartment is a duplex with the first level a half-flight up from the entry. The upper level of this unit contains a master bedroom and the living room which is on a balcony overlooking the two-story dining space.

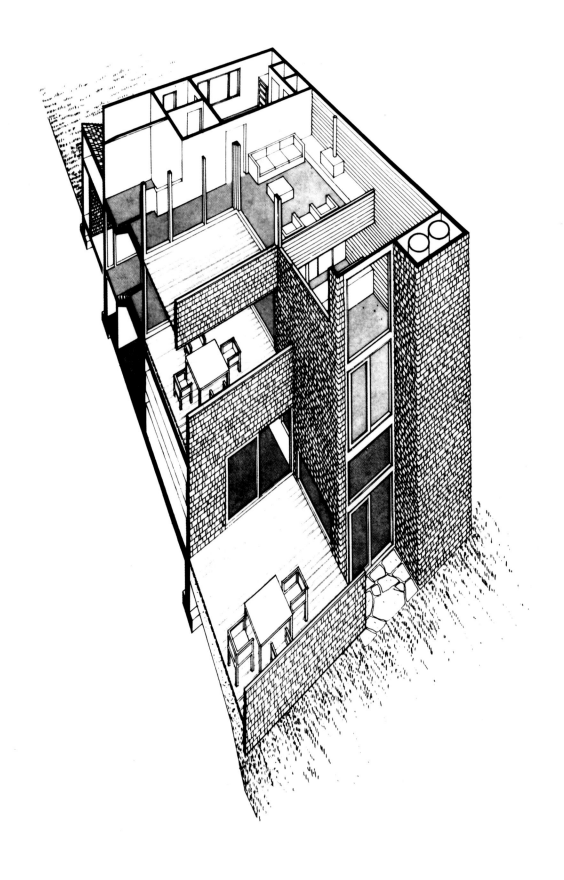

LE CHÂTEAU

Caption goes here

131

WESTOVER APARTMENTS
WASHINGTON, DC
PROJECT 1979

ecause one side of the property line is at a 45-degree angle to Massachusetts Avenue, the building is off-set at the core to develop the maximum allowable building length from side-yard to side-yard. Internally, this allows natural light to be introduced to the corridors at the central elevator core as well as at the ends of the building. Externally, the offset breaks down the length of the building and defines open areas which position the swimming pool and tennis facilities.

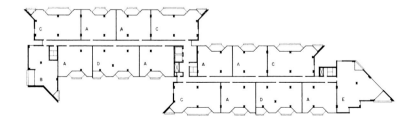

C TWO BEDROOM
1225 S.F.

A ONE BEDROOM
900.3 S.F.

133

PUBLIC

GENESEE CROSSROADS PLAZA
ROCHESTER, NEW YORK
1969

The plaza is located on a long, narrow 3-acre parcel that borders the Genesee river as it runs through the heart of the C.B.D. A 600-car underground garage was designed as a staggered-floor ramp system to facilitate a gradual stepping down of the plaza to the river. The resulting half-story difference in parking deck levels also provides continuous planting pockets of sufficient depth to accommodate full size trees.

The diagonal alignment of the pedestrian bridge connects with the Plaza directly in front of the underground garage stair tower. The diagonal configuration is further developed, through an additional leg, so that the bridge becomes an over-the-water extension of the plaza itself.

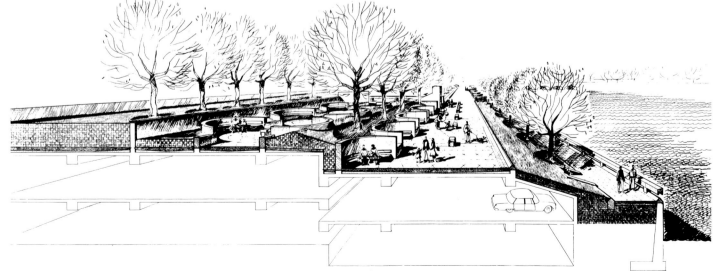

138

GIRL SCOUT DINING HALL
QUAKERTOWN, PA
1968

This summer camp dining hall was designed to accommodate 250 campers. To address problems of scale and acoustic control, the dining area was broken into two wings treated as screened porches that focus on a common amphitheater. These porches can be closed during the winter months or in inclement weather by side coiling partitions. Folding doors allow one of the dining wings and adjoining toilet facilities to be partitioned off from the rest of the structure for off-season troop camping.

Tongue-and-groove roof plank is framed into the upper and lower members of the truss running the length of the dining rooms allowing a continuous clerestory for light and ventilation.

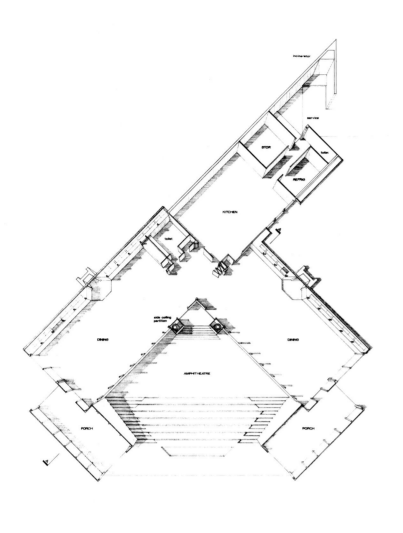

PERSPECTIVE PLAN

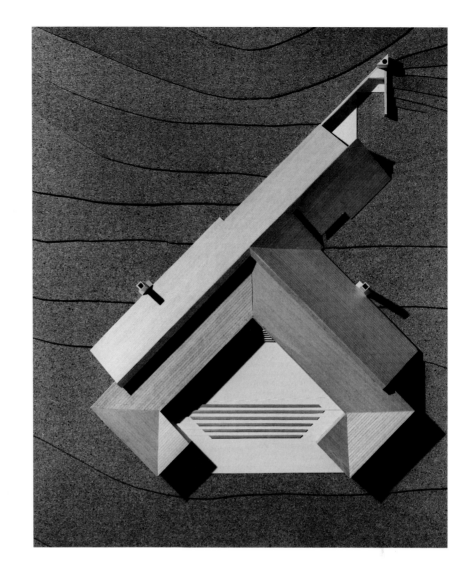

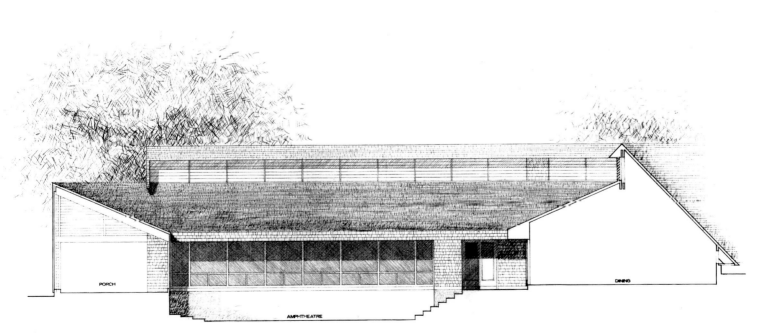

145

147

tight, urban site suggested a scheme wherein locker rooms and related areas were lowered a half level below grade and aligned along both sides of the pool. The inner walls of the locker rooms and pool thus "build" each other and the roof of the locker rooms becomes the pool deck located a half level above grade. In a sense, the building "disappears" in the total complex, allowing 100 percent utilization of the site for deck, pool and terrace areas.

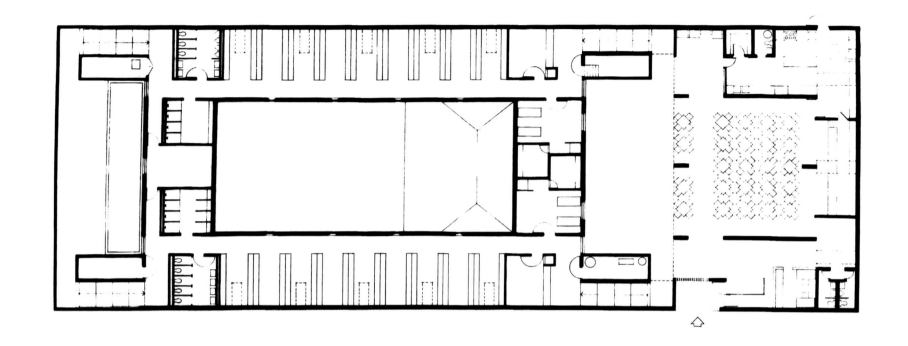

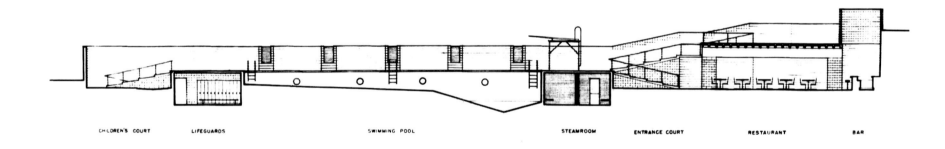

CHILDREN'S COURT   LIFEGUARDS   SWIMMING POOL   STEAMROOM   ENTRANCE COURT   RESTAURANT   BAR

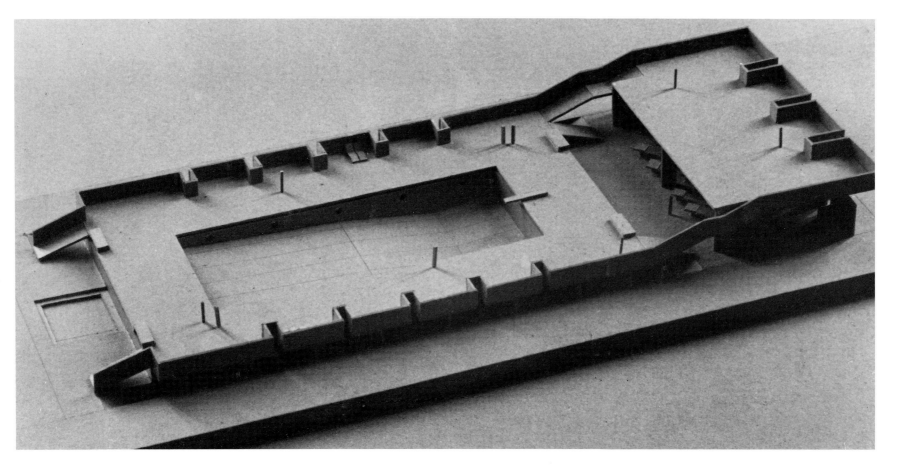

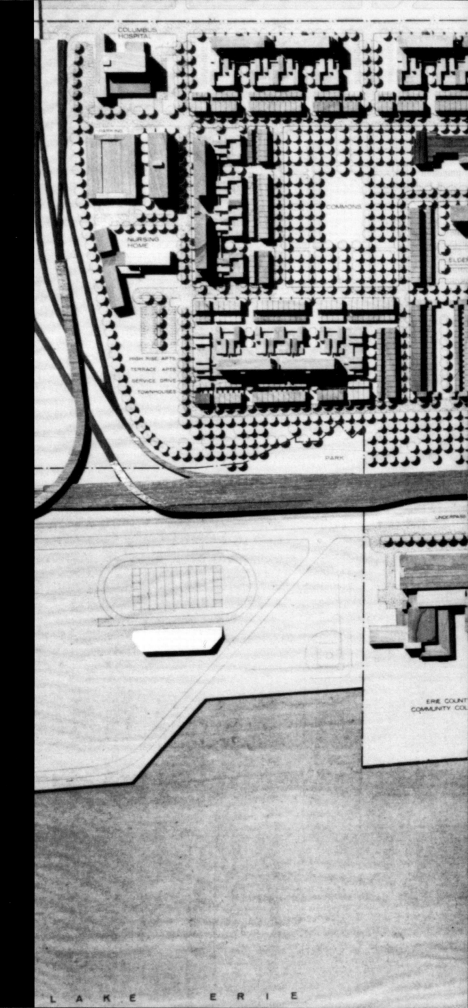

WATERFRONT REDEVELOPMENT
BUFFALO, NEW YORK
PROJECT 1967

A 293-acre project whose overall goal was to tie the development of the Lake Erie waterfront into the development of the Central Business District and adjoining residential areas.

In the area between Lake Erie and the Niagara Thruway, a 4000 student community college is proposed along with high density residential uses, a municipal marina, a boatel and supporting commercial facilities.

The area to the east of the Thruway is proposed for development as a self-contained neighborhood including mid-rise, terrace and garden apartments, town houses, shopping, church, school and recreational facilities.

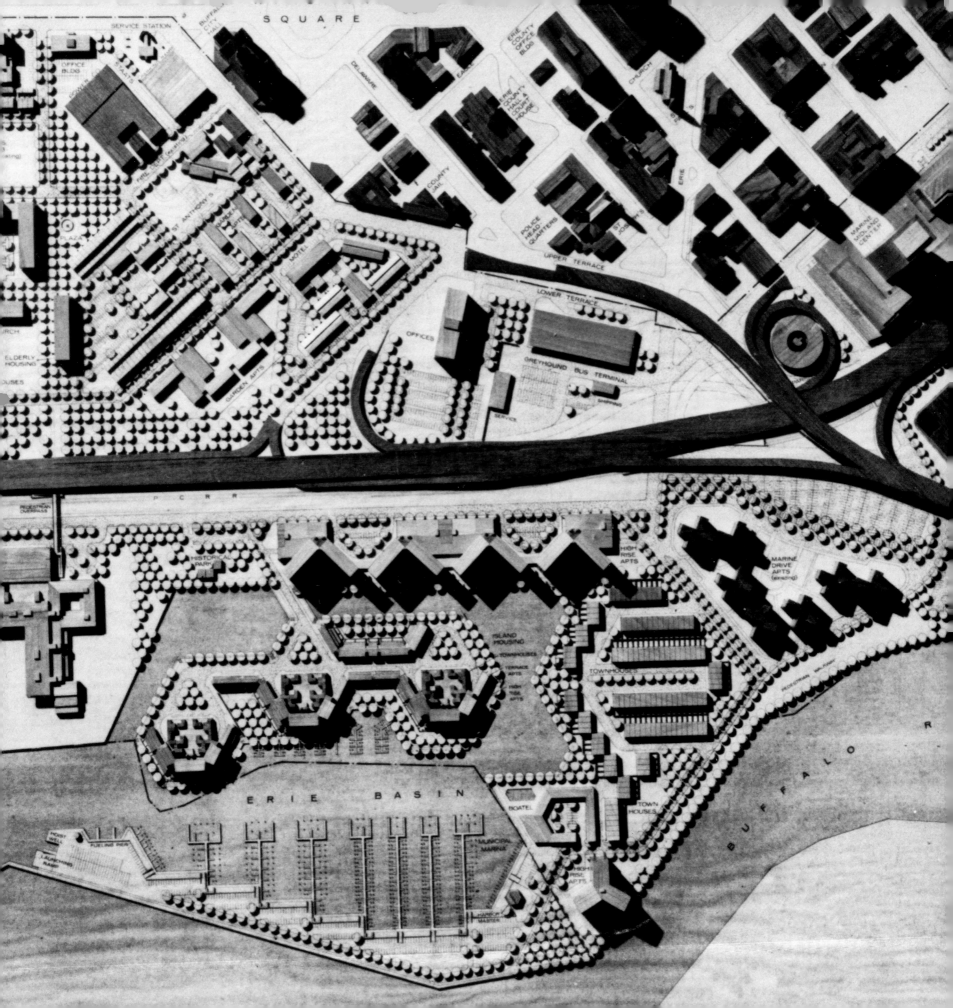

This facility, providing a gathering point for nature walks, lecture facilities and office space for park naturalists, is set away from the upper access level of the site. The entrance is across a bridge to the roof of the building which serves as an observation deck with views along a stream in two directions. An outside stair leads down to the office level and the lecture space. The building thus serves as a public stair from the parking area to the stream valley below. Construction is heavy wood framing covered with wood shingles.

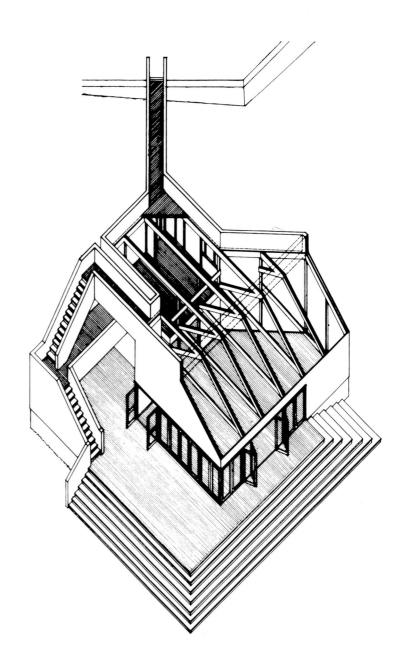

155

MERCER-JACKSON
REDEVELOPMENT TRENTON, N.J.
PROJECT 1965

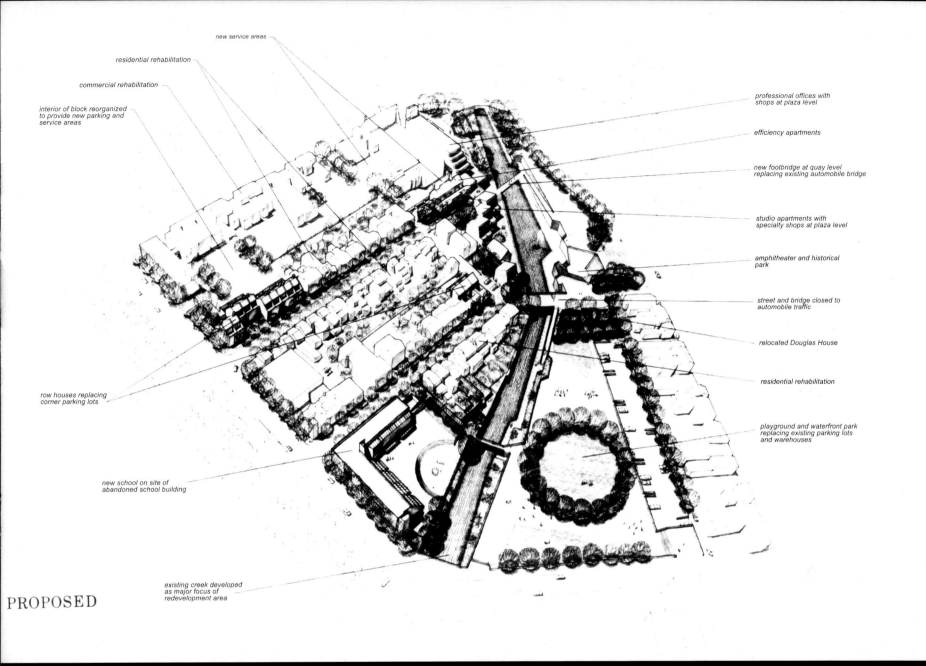

new service areas

residential rehabilitation

commercial rehabilitation

interior of block reorganized
to provide new parking and
service areas

professional offices with
shops at plaza level

efficiency apartments

new footbridge at quay level
replacing existing automobile bridge

studio apartments with
specialty shops at plaza level

amphitheater and historical
park

street and bridge closed to
automobile traffic

relocated Douglas House

residential rehabilitation

row houses replacing
corner parking lots

playground and waterfront park
replacing existing parking lots
and warehouses

new school on site of
abandoned school building

existing creek developed
as major focus of
redevelopment area

PROPOSED

This 22-acre site, conveniently located near the down-town business district and state office complex, has great potential as a center city residential area.

The Assunpink Creek, presently lined by warehouse and parking facilities and, therefore, lost to the city as an amenity, is seen as the public generator for the rehabilitation of the area. It is proposed that the city construct quays, sitting areas, and a small park along its banks as well as an elementary school and playground straddling the creek and connected by a pedestrian bridge.

Housing is to be furnished primarily by rehabilitation of existing structures. Any proposed new housing takes place on what are now parking lots, eliminating relocation problems.

To encourage public usage, new construction along the northern end of the creek proposes shops at ground level along the quay with office and apartment accommodations above.

RESIDENTIAL

ORITSKY RESIDENCE
READING, PA

The site is on the corner of a residential street with a 20-foot change in grade from the street corner to its low point. To give privacy from the streets and surrounding houses, the house is nestled into the natural bowl formed by the topography. For further privacy, the house is organized around a courtyard that acts as both an entry court and a flat, shielded outdoor area for the adult activities that occur on this main level. The lower level contains the wife's studio, children's' bedrooms and playroom that opens to its own outdoor area.

Because of its low elevation in relation to the adjoining streets, the roof is treated as a major formal element of the building—a "fifth" façade.

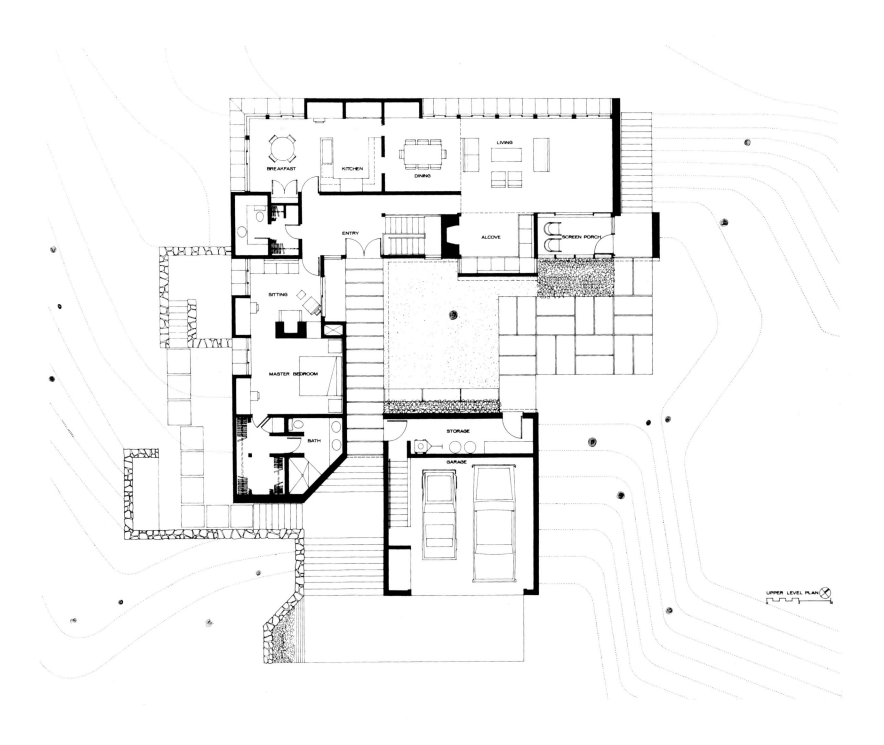

BREAKFAST

KITCHEN

DINING

LIVING

ENTRY

ALCOVE

SCREEN PORCH

SITTING

MASTER BEDROOM

BATH

STORAGE

GARAGE

UPPER LEVEL PLAN

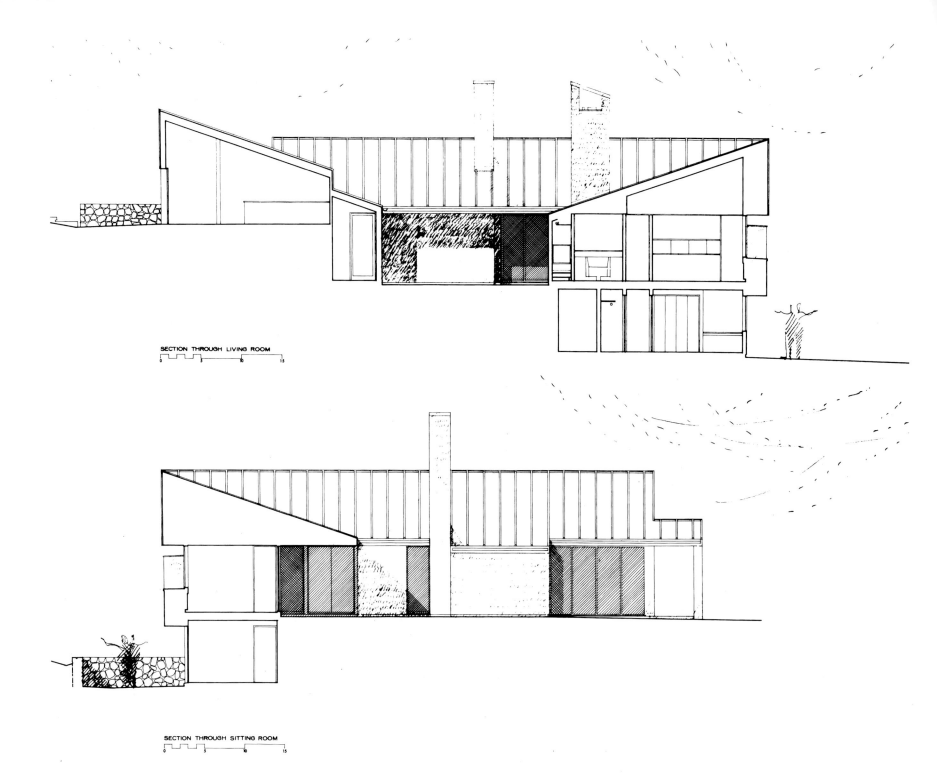

SECTION THROUGH LIVING ROOM

0   5   10   15

SECTION THROUGH SITTING ROOM

0   5   10   15

LEMMON RESIDENCE
GLADWYNE, PA
1967

This house, on a steeply sloping site, utilizes a series of wings acting, in effect, as retaining walls to create two flat areas.

The first is a children's courtyard created by backing the children's bedroom wing into the slope to create a play area. The other is the motor court created by utilizing the lowest level of the house as a retaining wall. The upper level of the house contains the children's' wing, separated from the master bedroom by the court and playroom. The entry and owner's study is also located at this level. The lower level accommodates the living and dining areas as well as the kitchen and maid's room.

BLUMENTHAL RESIDENCE I
PRINCETON, NEW JERSEY
PROJECT 1962

T he steeply sloping site overlooking Lake Carnegie was complicated by a 20-foot-wide sewer easement running diagonally across it.

The formal organization of the house centers around a connecting bridge over this easement and a 120-degree module, both of which were the direct result of site considerations. The module made possible an ever-changing series of lake vistas from the bedrooms and entrance gallery as well as providing direct supervision of the swimming pool area from the kitchen, located on the connecting bridge.

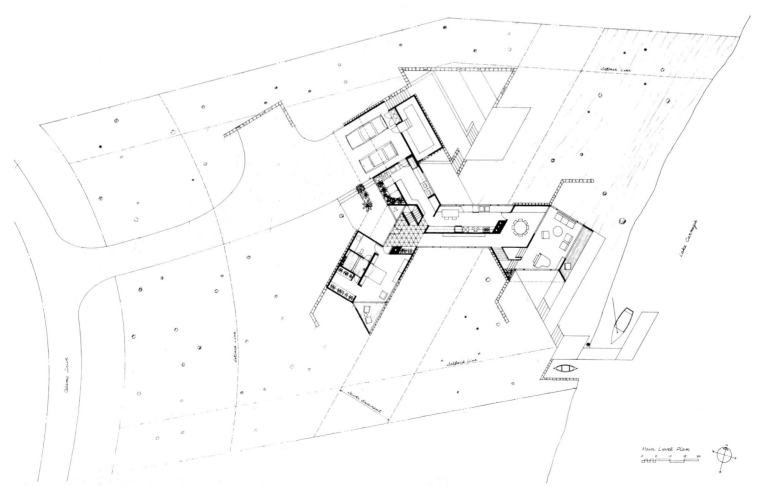

Main Level Plan

BLUMENTHAL RESIDENCE II
PRINCETON, NEW JERSEY
1964

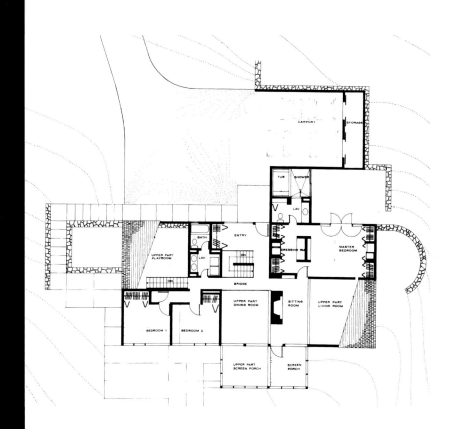

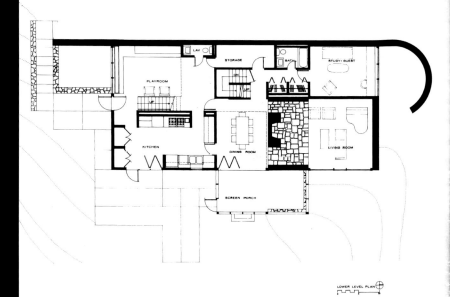

LOWER LEVEL PLAN

The main entrance of the house is at the upper level, with the master bedroom suite on one side of the entry and the children's bedrooms on the other. The upper portions of the living room, dining room and playroom penetrate this upper level allowing views of the living room and dining room from the sitting room balcony and giving direct access to the playroom from the children' bedrooms. The lower level contains the main living areas as well as a study/guest room.

SCHLESINGER RESIDENCE
BUCKS COUNTY, PA
1960

An inward looking plan, with the required smaller spaces of the house pulled out to the building's perimeter, thus screening the larger, living spaces that are left free on the interior, answers to the demands of a small corner lot in a residential neighborhood. Active family functions take place on the lower level while the upper level is given over to adult activities. A top lite, double-height dining room acts as the ceremonial heart of the house.

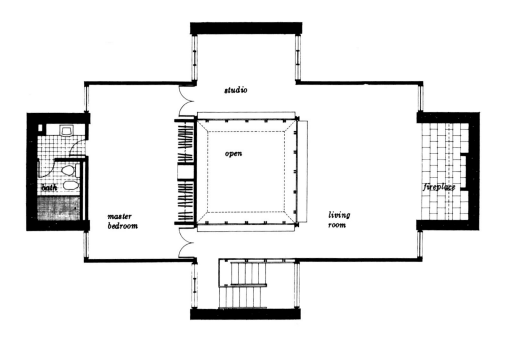

Upper Level Plan

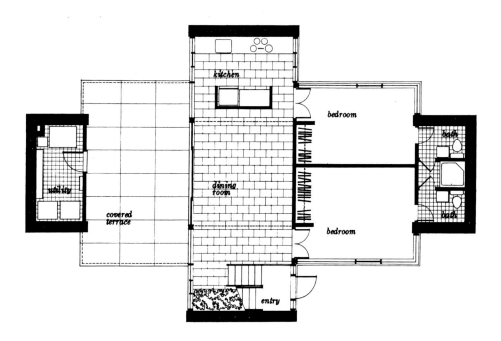

Lower Level Plan

180

BERNSTEIN/SPAR RESIDENCE
PRINCETON, NJ
1958 & 1990

NORTH ELEVATION

0 2 4   8

WEST ELEVATION

0 2 4   8

This is an addition to a house done by this firm 30 years before. The original house was designed for a narrow sloping site overlooking a brook to the north. Its entrance and main living areas are on the upper level with the bedrooms below opening to the lower portion of the site. The house was organized structurally and spatially around four masonry piers that rise unbroken from grade to the roof line.

tion to incorporate a clerestory in place of the original skylight lost to the addition. As opposed to the original structure's flat roof, the copper sheathed roof of the addition is manipulated in response to the need for an "attic" to accommodate new air conditioning ductwork.

SCHLESINGER RESIDENCE
LEXINGTON, MA
1954

In this minimum house for a family of four, an effort was made to incorporate as much spatial variety, changing light quality and varied outlook as possible within the confines of approximately 1,000 square feet. Transitional areas on three sides of the house aid in enlarging it visually as well as physically. A screened terrace serves as extension for the living room during the greater part of the year, while an adjoining flower gar-

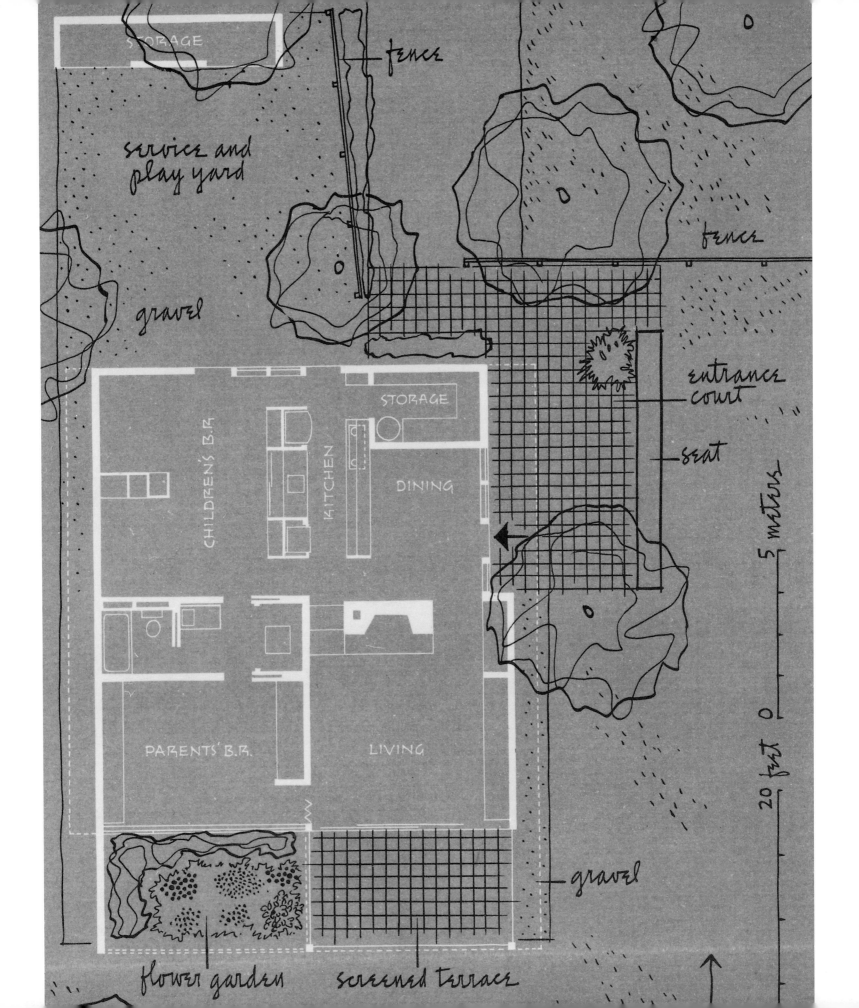

STORAGE

fence

service and
play yard

gravel

CHILDREN'S B.R.

KITCHEN

STORAGE

DINING

fence

entrance
court

seat

PARENTS' B.R.

LIVING

gravel

flower garden

screened terrace

20 feet   0   5 meters

185

A 20-foot deed easement parallel to the street established a triangular buildable area of 1000 square feet. Rather than making the building envelope coincident with this easement, the building is configured as a series of orthogonal setbacks within this line, giving better definition to interior rooms while, at the same time, creating more usable outdoor areas.

The house is organized spatially around a two story dining room. Water views afforded by a roof terrace make it the most important private, outdoor living space of the house. A small studio is also located on this level.

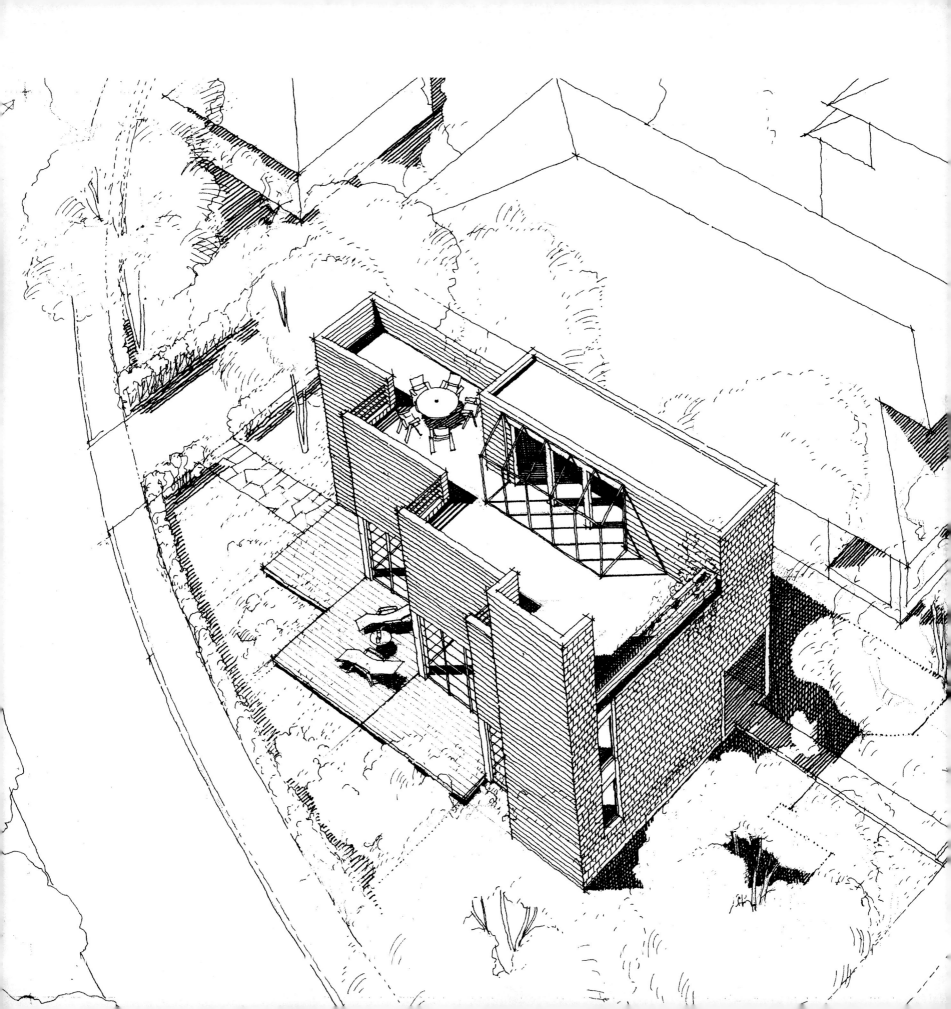

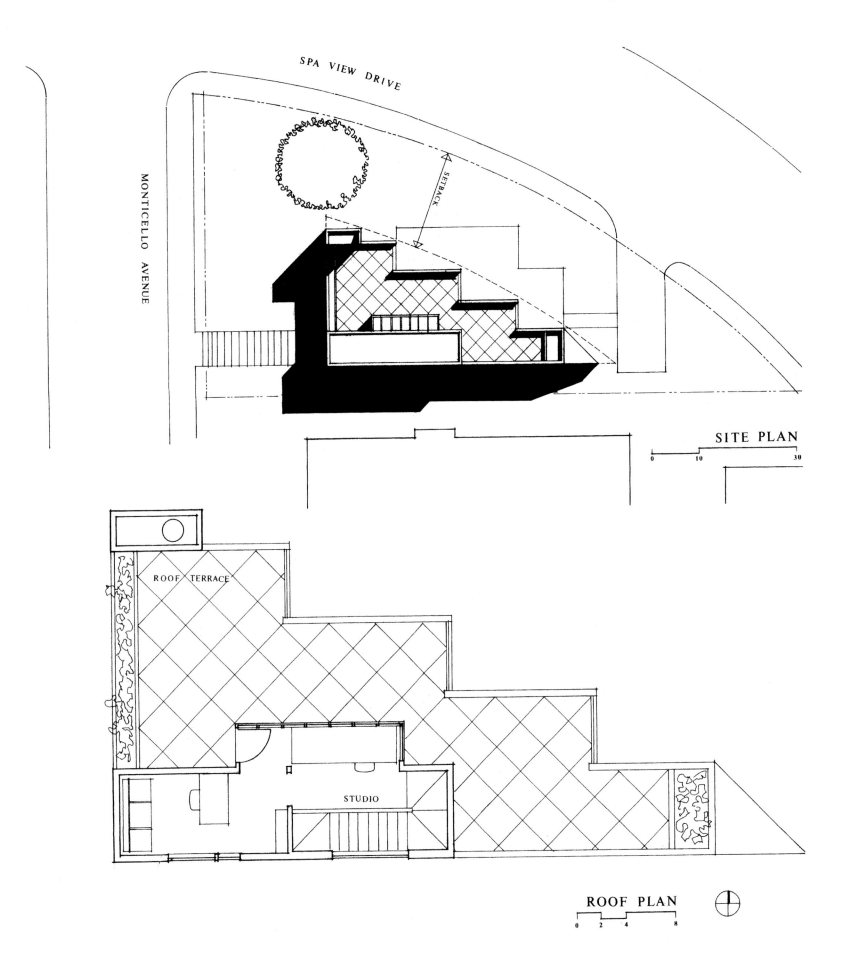

SPA VIEW DRIVE

MONTICELLO AVENUE

SETBACK

SITE PLAN

0   10   30

ROOF TERRACE

STUDIO

ROOF PLAN

0 2 4   8

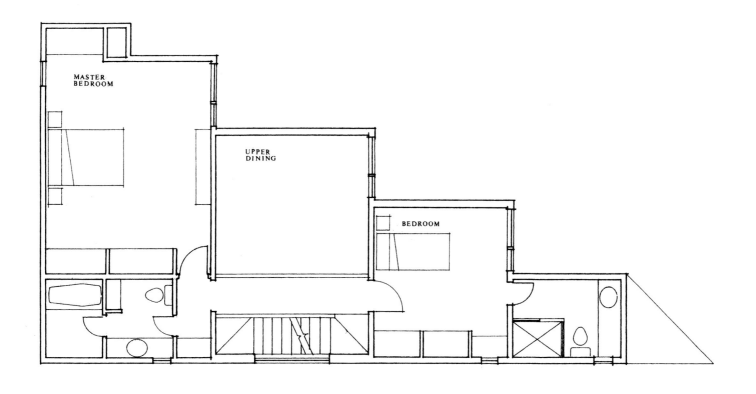

SECOND FLOOR PLAN

0 2 4 8

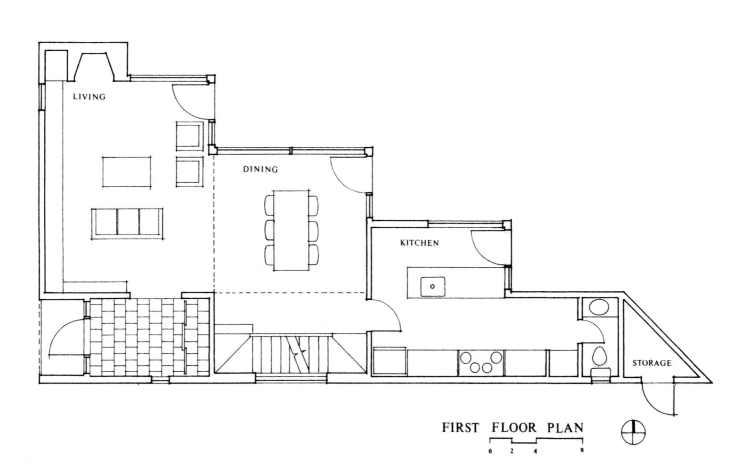

FIRST FLOOR PLAN

0 2 4 8

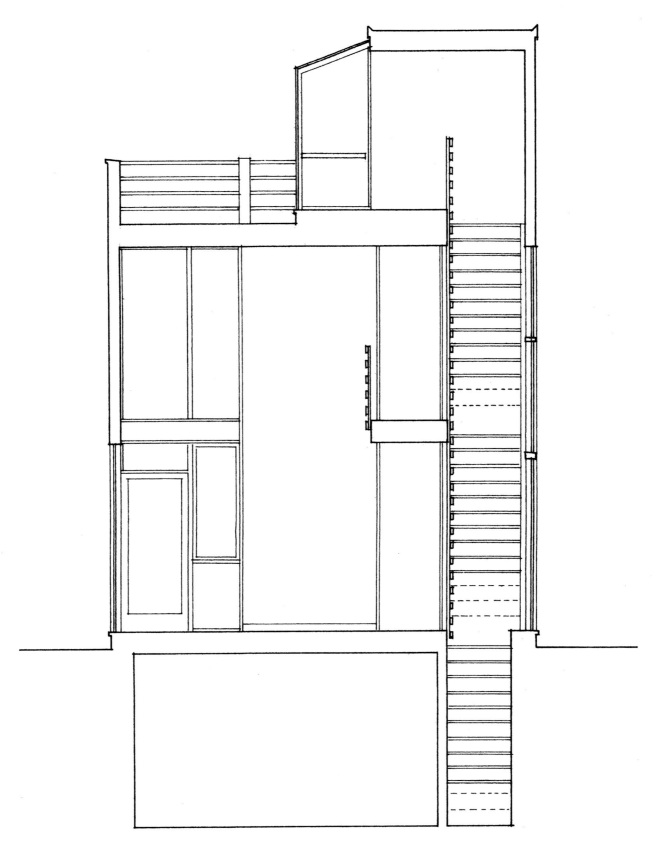

SECTION at DINING ROOM

MALKEIL RESIDENCE
PRINCETON, N.J.
PROJECT1968

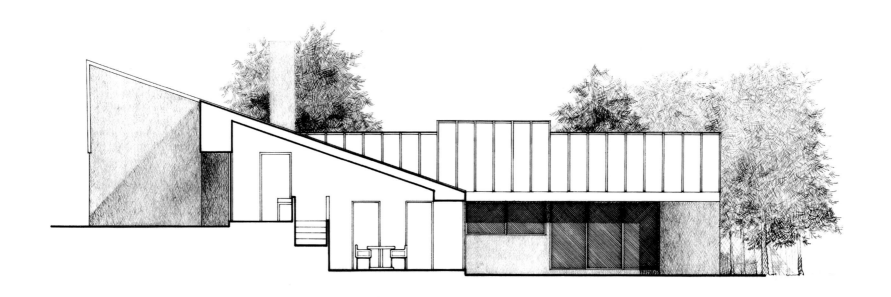

SECTION THRU DINING ROOM

0 5 10 15

SECTION THRU LIVING ROOM

0 5 10 15

194

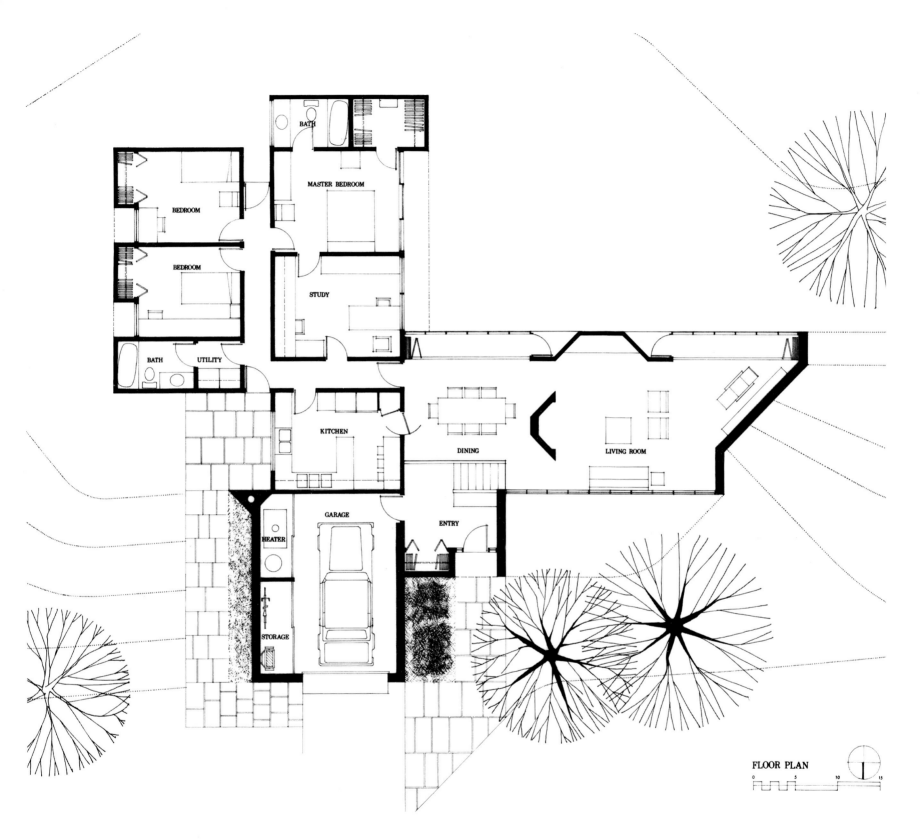

BATH

MASTER BEDROOM

BEDROOM

BEDROOM

STUDY

BATH

UTILITY

KITCHEN

DINING

LIVING ROOM

HEATER

GARAGE

ENTRY

STORAGE

FLOOR PLAN

0   5   10   15

This residence required unusual facilities for entertaining and overnight guests. Six guest rooms and their lounge were placed around a courtyard on the lower level. Their roofs form a series of terraces for the main living spaces above. Entry to the house is from a porte-cochere to a large, skylit reception area. All major living spaces are reached from this area. A master bedroom suite, with private access to the main floor library, is located on the upper level.

The requirement for a nine car garage was resolved by distributing the spaces among three structures, two of which are sunk into the sloping site to form a flat motor court, while the third becomes the central element of a turn-around and the terminus of the porte-cochere.

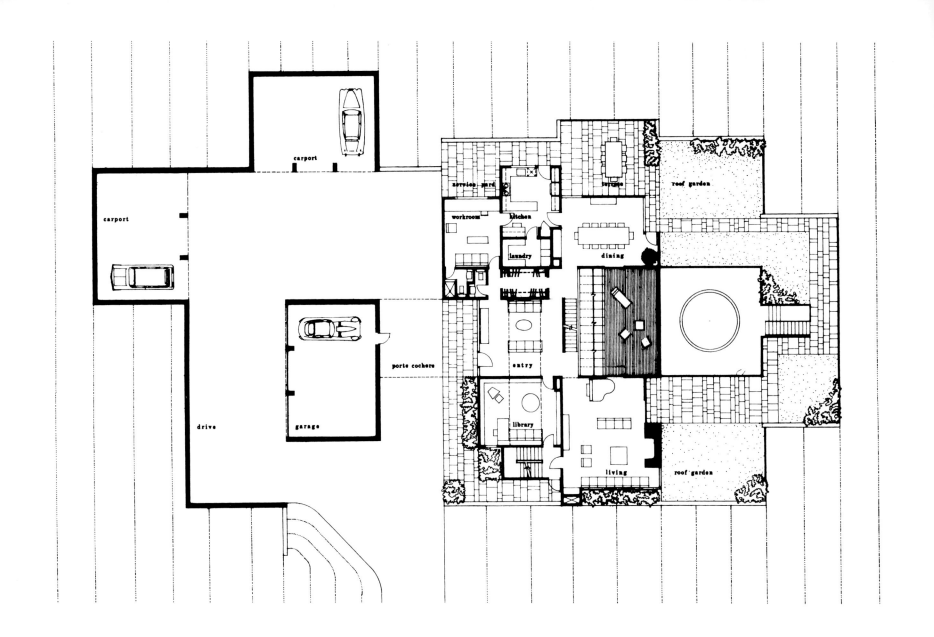

carport

carport

drive

porte cochere

garage

service yard

workroom

kitchen

laundry

dining

terrace

roof garden

entry

library

living

roof garden

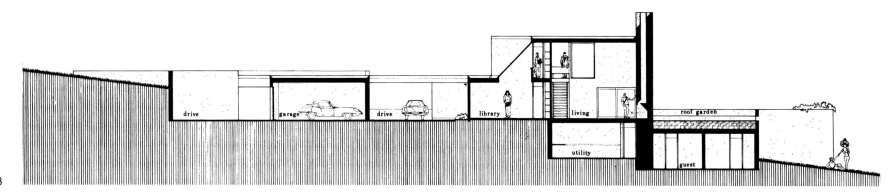

drive

garage

drive

library

living

roof garden

utility

guest

198

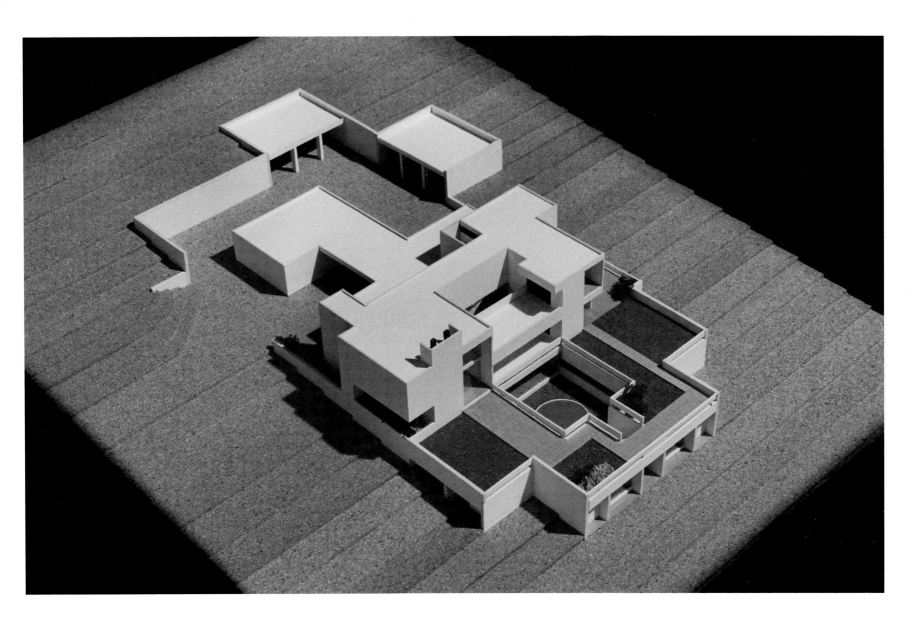

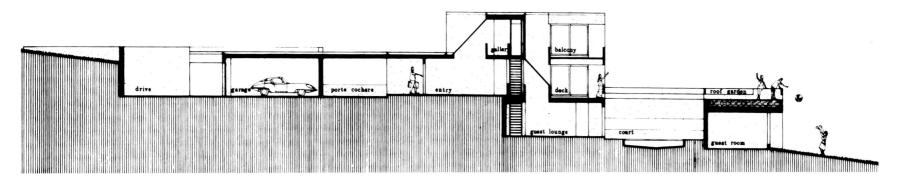

drive garage porte cochere entry gallery balcony deck roof garden guest lounge court guest room

TUBULAR STEEL RESIDENCE
NORRISTOWN, PA
PROJECT 1965

This house was designed for a fabricator of tubular steel products. Making the most of the structural properties of tubular steel, two 63-foot trusses cantilever 21 feet from both ends of three central supporting bays. Beams span between these trusses and from them are hung the floor structure of the dining room, living room and master bedroom. The two story dining room and deck cantilever over the slope, while the hung master bedroom provides a carport underneath. The upper level contains the living room and master bedroom. The lower level houses the children's rooms. Family activities come together on the middle level where the dining room and kitchen are located.

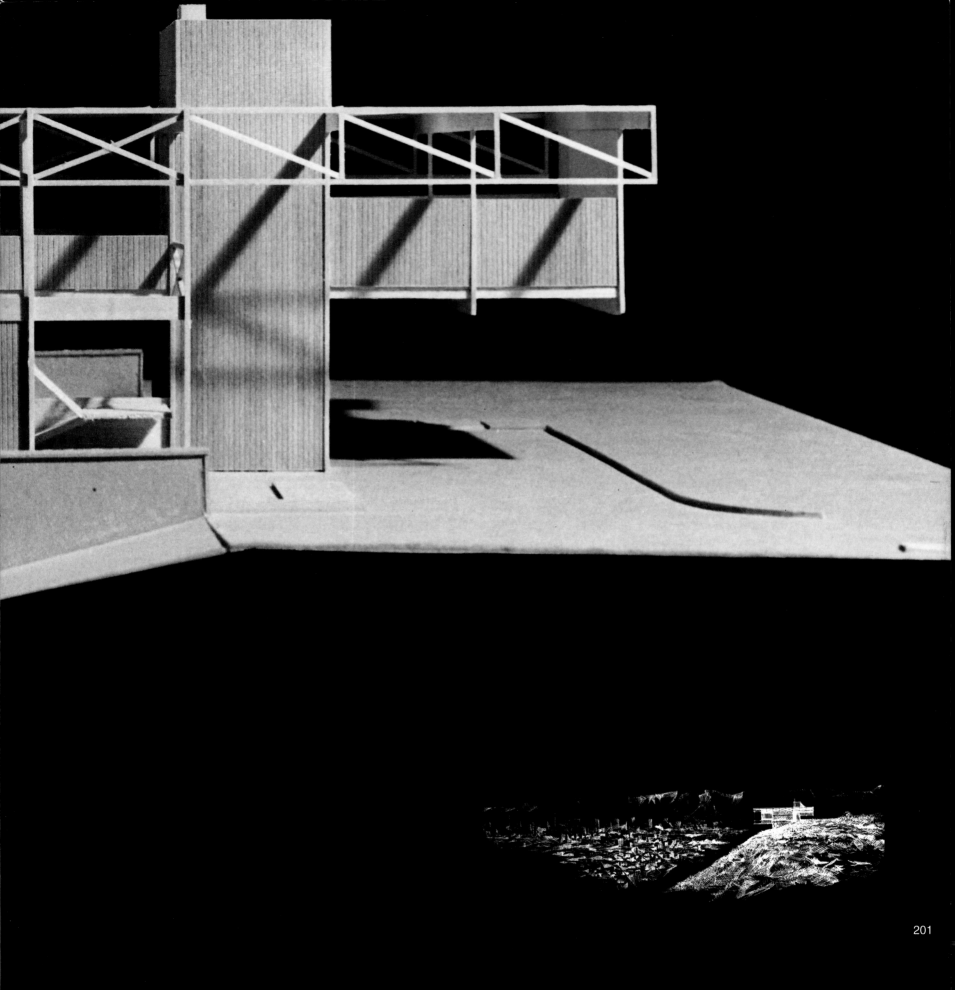

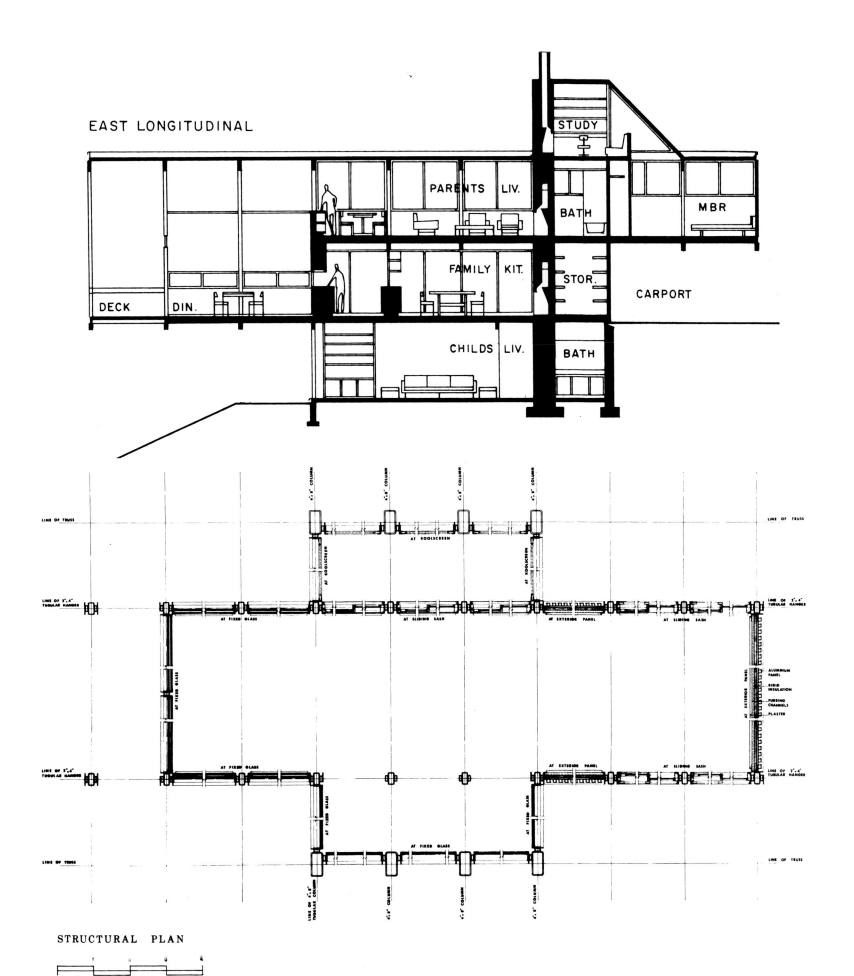

EAST LONGITUDINAL

STUDY

PARENTS LIV.

BATH

MBR

DECK DIN.

FAMILY KIT.

STOR.

CARPORT

CHILDS LIV.

BATH

LINE OF TRUSS

LINE OF TRUSS

4'-8" COLUMN

4'-8" COLUMN

4'-8" COLUMN

4'-8" COLUMN

AT KOOLSCREEN

AT KOOLSCREEN

AT KOOLSCREEN

AT KOOLSCREEN

LINE OF 3'-4"
TUBULAR HANGER

LINE OF 3'-4"
TUBULAR HANGER

AT FIXED GLASS

AT SLIDING SASH

AT EXTERIOR PANEL

AT SLIDING SASH

AT FIXED GLASS

AT FIXED GLASS

ALUMINUM
PANEL

RIGID
INSULATION

FURRING
CHANNELS

PLASTER

AT EXTERIOR PANEL

LINE OF 3'-4"
TUBULAR HANGER

AT FIXED GLASS

AT EXTERIOR PANEL

AT SLIDING SASH

LINE OF 3'-4"
TUBULAR HANGER

AT FIXED GLASS

AT FIXED GLASS

LINE OF TRUSS

AT FIXED GLASS

LINE OF TRUSS

LINE OF 4'-8"
TUBULAR COLUMN

4'-8" COLUMN

4'-8" COLUMN

4'-8" COLUMN

STRUCTURAL PLAN

COURTYARDS
SACRED AND PROFANE

This figure-ground drawing illustrates a series of projects–all drawn at the same scale–that demonstrate my on-going interest in the idea of "courtyard" as the basis for spacemaking. The idea is a simple one and one that has manifested itself from the classic world of the Mediterranean to the Scandinavia of Aalto and Utzon: in contrast to a building floating in a sea of infinite space, the idea of courtyard can "pin" a building spatially to a specific place. By allowing a building, or a complex of buildings, to envelop a piece of finite space and it can make that space imageable rather than diffuse, usable rather than residual. Courtyards also allow a wonderful degree of flexibility. Their outside perimeter can accommodate a variety of forms and uses that are held together compositionally by the clarity of the courtyard space itself, which acts as the prime "room" and organizational armature of the building complex.

—F.S.

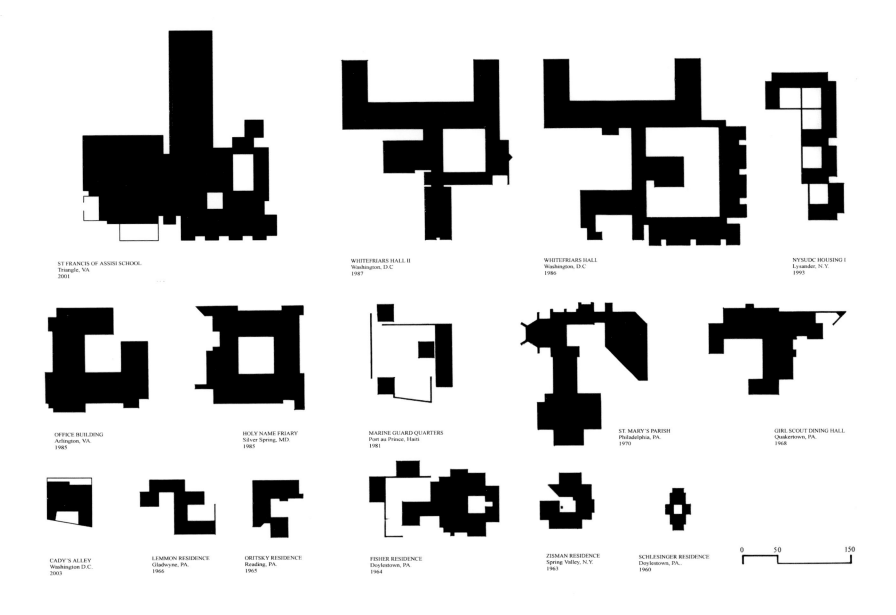

ST FRANCIS OF ASSISI SCHOOL.
Triangle, VA
2001

WHITEFRIARS HALL II
Washington, D.C
1987

WHITEFRIARS HALL
Washington, D.C
1986

NYSUDC HOUSING I
Lysander, N.Y.
1993

OFFICE BUILDING
Arlington, VA.
1985

HOLY NAME FRIARY
Silver Spring, MD.
1985

MARINE GUARD QUARTERS
Port au Prince, Haiti
1981

ST. MARY'S PARISH
Philadelphia, PA.
1970

GIRL SCOUT DINING HALL
Quakertown, PA.
1968

CADY'S ALLEY
Washington D.C.
2003

LEMMON RESIDENCE
Gladwyne, PA.
1966

ORITSKY RESIDENCE
Reading, PA.
1965

FISHER RESIDENCE
Doylestown, PA.
1964

ZISMAN RESIDENCE
Spring Valley, N.Y.
1963

SCHLESINGER RESIDENCE
Doylestown, PA..
1960

0   50   150

FRANK SCHLESINGER
PROFILE

EDUCATION

1950-54 Master of Architecture
  Graduate School of Design
  Harvard University
  Cambridge, Massachusetts
1948-50 Bachelor of Science
  University of Illinois
  Champaign-Urbana, Illinois
1946-48 Middlebury College
  Middlebury, Vermont

PROFESSIONAL PRACTICE

1956-Present—Principal
  Frank Schlesinger Architects
1959-60 Staff
  Louis Kahn, Architect
  Philadelphia, Pennsylvania
1955-56 Staff
  Marcel Breuer, Architect
  New York, New York
1953-55 Staff
  Hugh Stubbins, Architect
  Cambridge, Massachusetts

HONORS AND FELLOWSHIPS

2001 Centennial Medal
  Washington Chapter
  American Institute of Architects
1984 Distinguished Designer Sabbatical Fellowship
  National Endowment for the Arts
  Washington, DC
1971 Kea Distinguished Professor
  School of Architecture
  University of Maryland
  College Park, Maryland
1970 Fellow
  American Institute of Architects
1963 Arthur Wheelright Fellow in Architecture
  Graduate School of Design
  Harvard University
  Cambridge, Massachusetts

TEACHING

1971-2001 Professor of Architecture, Emeritus
  School of Architecture
  University of Maryland
  College Park, Maryland
1971 Kea Distinguished Professor
  School of Architecture
  University of Maryland
  College Park, Maryland
1965 Visiting Critic of Architecture
  Graduate School of Fine Arts
  University of Pennsylvania
  Philadelphia, Pennsylvania
1962-63 Adjunct Assistant Professor of Architecture
  School of Architecture
  Columbia University
  New York, New York
1957-60 Instructor in Architecture
  School of Fine Arts
  University of Pennsylvania
  Philadelphia, Pennsylvania

DESIGN AWARDS

2005 National Design Award
  American Institute of Architects
  Cady's Alley Redevelopment
  (In association with, Baranes, MacInturff, Sorg, Martinez, and Johnson)
2002 Design Award
  Washington Chapter
  American Institute of Architects
  St. Francis of Assisi Parish Center
2000 Design Award
  Northern Virginia Chapter
  American Institute of Architects
  St. Francis of Assisi Parish Center
1995 Design Award
  Washington Chapter
  American Institute of Architects
  Whitefriars Hall
  Washington, DC
1992 International Honor Award
  Interfaith Forum on Religion, Art and Architecture
  Whitefriars Hall
  Washington, DC
1992 Merit Award
  Washington Chapter

American Institute of Architects
  Holy Name Franciscan Friary
  Montgomery County, Maryland
1990 Merit Award
  Washington Chapter
  American Institute of Architects
  National Place/1331 Pennsylvania Avenue
  Office/Retail/Parking Complex
  Washington, DC
  (in association with Mitchell/Giurgola)
1987 Merit Award
  Interfaith Forum on Religion, Art and Architecture
  Holy Name Franciscan Friary
  Montgomery County, Maryland
1984 Honor Award
  Pennsylvania Society of Architects
  National Place/1331 Pennsylvania Avenue
  Hotel/Office/Retail Complex
  Washington, DC
  (in association with Mitchell/Giurgola)
1975 Honor Award
  Northern Virginia Chapter
  American Institute of Architects
  Freedom Valley Girl Scout Dining Hall
  Bucks County, Pennsylvania
    Honor Award
  Northern Virginia Chapter
  American Institute of Architects
  Christy Village Condominiums
  Beech Mountain, North Carolina
1974 Design Award
  Architectural Record
  Record Houses of 1974
  Christy Village Condominiums
  Beech Mountain, North Carolina
    Design Award
  Progressive Architecture
  St. Mary's at the Cathedral
  Philadelphia, Pennsylvania
1973 Silver Medal
  Pennsylvania Society of Architects
  Housing for the Elderly
  Bristol, Pennsylvania
  (in association with Louis Sauer)
1972 Design Award
  Progressive Architecture
  Residence

Norristown, Pennsylvania
1970 Award of Merit
  Homes for Better Living
  American Institute of Architects and
  House and Home
  Residence
  Reading, Pennsylvania
1969 Citation for Excellence
  Philadelphia Chapter
  American Institute of Architects
  Office Building Fountains, Inc.
  South Coventry, Connecticut
    Distinguished Building Award
  Pennsylvania Society of Architects
  Residence
  Reading, Pennsylvania
    Design Award
  Progressive Architecture
  Nature Center, Fairmount Park
  Philadelphia, Pennsylvania
1968 Citation for Excellence
  Philadelphia Chapter
  American Institute of Architects
  Freedom Valley Girl Scout Dining Hall
  Bucks County, Pennsylvania
1967 Design Award
  Progressive Architecture
  Genesee Crossroads Plaza
  Rochester, New York
1966 Design Award
  Progressive Architecture
  Mercer-Jackson Redevelopment Area
  Trenton, New Jersey
1965 Bronze Medal
  Pennsylvania Society of Architects
  Mercer-Jackson Redevelopment Area
  Trenton, New Jersey
    Citation for Excellence
  Pennsylvania Society of Architects
  American Institute of Architects
  Mercer-Jackson Redevelopment Area
  Trenton, New Jersey
    Citation for Excellence
  Pennsylvania Society of Architects
  American Institute of Architects
  Medical Offices
  Bristol, Pennsylvania

    Honor Award
  Pennsylvania Society of Architects
  Residence
  Reading, Pennsylvania
1964 Benjamin Franklin Medal
  Producers Council Award
  Philadelphia Chapter
  American Institute of Architects
  Pavilion, Beachcomber Swim Club
  Norristown, Pennsylvania
  (in association with TR Vreeland)
    Citation for Excellence
  Philadelphia Chapter
  American Institute of Architects
  Pavilion, Beachcomber Swim Club
  Norristown, Pennsylvania
  (in association with TR Vreeland)
    Honor Award
  Pennsylvania Society of Architects
  Pavilion, Beachcomber Swim Club
  Norristown, Pennsylvania
  (in association with TR Vreeland)
    Honor Award
  Pennsylvania Society of Architects
  Residence
  Spring Valley, New York
1963 Citation for Excellence
  Philadelphia Chapter
  American Institute of Architects
  Residence
  Norristown, Pennsylvania
    Honor Award
  Pennsylvania Society of Architects
  Residence
  Princeton, New Jersey
1962 Benjamin Franklin Medal
  Producers Council Award
  Philadelphia Chapter
  American Institute of Architects
  Camp Structure
  Quakertown, Pennsylvania
    Citation for Excellence
  Philadelphia Chapter
  American Institute of Architects
  Residence
  Princeton, New Jersey
1961 Citation for Excellence
  Philadelphia Chapter

American Institute of Architects
Rsidence
Princeton, New Jersey
   Honor Award
Pennsylvania Society of Architects
Rittenhouse Swim Club
Philadelphia, Pennsylvania
(in association with TR Vreeland)
   Honor Award
Pennsylvania Society of Architects
Residence
Princeton, New Jersey
   Design Award
Architectural Record
Record Houses of 1961
Residence
Doylestown, Pennsylvania
1960 Citation for Excellence
Philadelphia Chapter
American Institute of Architects
Residence
Doylestown, Pennsylvania

EXHIBITS

1998 "Frank Schlesinger, Architect"
  A Retrospective
  University of Maryland, College Park, Maryland
1979 "The Federal City in Transition"
  The Barbara Fiedler Gallery
  Washington, DC
1968 "Frank Schlesinger, Architect"
  Philadelphia Art Alliance
  Philadelphia, Pennsylvania
1965 "40 Under 40"
  Architectural League of New York
  New York, New York
1963 Exhibition
  National Gold Medal Exhibit
  Architectural League of New York
  New York, New York

STAFF AND COLLEAGUES

PRINCETON, N.J.
  Elizabeth Moynahan
  Jeanne Schlesinger

DOYLESTOWN, PA.
  Atillio Bergamasco
  Ralph Bolton
  Fred Foote
  Richard Hamner
  Elizabeth Lawson
  John Lawson
  Marshall Meyers
  Reginald Richey
  Joan Roberts
  Jeanne Schlesinger
  Mark Spitzer
  Patricia Statts
  Robert Weimer

PHILADELPHIA, PA.
  Harold Guida
  Reginald Richey
  Lee Tollefson

WASHINGTON, D.C.
  Attillio Bergamasco
  Joseph Boggs
  Reginald Richey
  Draga Schlesinger
  Jeff Schlesinger
  Richard Thorp

RESTON, VA.
  Steven Chin
  Graham Davidson
  Bora Popovitch

WASHINGTON, D.C.
  Kim Armour
  Britt Brewer
  Beth Buffington
  Steven Chin
  Phillip Eagleburger
  Cynthia Frank
  Alan Greenberger
  Brooke Harington
  Hyun Kim
  Larysa Kurylas
  Michael Levy
  Paul Loh
  Iris Miller
  Yves Mudry
  Robert Oberdorf
  Antonio Rebelo
  Tracy Revis
  David Ricks
  Christy Schlesinger
  Draga Schlesinger
  Adrian Umansky
  Randy Wagner
  Gregory Wiedemann
  Joanne Young

PHOTO CREDITS